GETTING THE
RIGHT JOB

A PERSONAL GUIDE TO DEVELOPING YOUR CAREER

FOUNTAINHEAD
PRESS

Our green initiatives include:

Electronic Products

We deliver products in non-paper form whenever possible. This includes pdf downloadables, flash drives, and CDs.

Electronic Samples

We use Xample, a new electronic sampling system. Instructor samples are sent via a personalized web page that links to pdf downloads.

FSC Certified Printers

All of our printers are certified by the Forest Service Council, which promotes environmentally and socially responsible management of the world's forests. This program allows consumer groups, individual consumers, and businesses to work together hand-in-hand to promote responsible use of the world's forests as a renewable and sustainable resource.

Recycled Paper

Most of our products are printed on a minimum of 30% post-consumer waste recycled paper.

Support of Green Causes

When we do print, we donate a portion of our revenue to green causes. Listed below are a few of the organizations that have received donations from Fountainhead Press. We welcome your feedback and suggestions for contributions, as we are always searching for worthy initiatives.

    Rainforest 2 Reef

    Environmental Working Group

Designer: Lori Bryan

Copyright © 2016 Frank Munson
A previous edition of this book was published by Pearson Education, Inc.

Books may be purchased for educational purposes. For information, please call or write:
    1-800-586-0330
    Fountainhead Press
    Southlake, TX 76092
    Web site: www.fountainheadpress.com
    E-mail: customerservice@fountainheadpress.com

ISBN: 978-1-68036-330-2
Printed in the United States of America

ACKNOWLEDGMENTS

The authors and editors of this book would like to thank Dr. Felipe Thomaz, Assistant Professor of Marketing at the Darla Moore School of Business, University of South Carolina, for providing content about social media and its uses in the job search process throughout the book. We genuinely appreciate his time, talent, and commitment to this project.

It is also with a heavy heart that we say goodbye to our co-author, Professor John Stern, Distinguished Lecturer in the Management Department at the Darla Moore School of Business, University of South Carolina. John passed away June 11, 2016 at his home in Chapin, SC after a short illness. His contribution to the content of this book, his passion for career management education, and his love for students were inspirational.

John, you were a great man, a good friend, and an amazing mentor. Your integrity, grit, and camaraderie will be sorely missed. Rest in peace, friend.

PREFACE

Why do we need a new approach, workbook, or textbook and commitment to achieving a higher success in:

- Graduation rates
- Graduation in 4 years instead of 6
- Preparing students / job seekers for job placement at graduation
- Helping unemployed and underemployed students / job seekers get the right jobs leading to more rewarding and meaningful careers

It is not a question of whether or not we are preparing students / job seekers for careers. It is a question of can we change to improve our results.

"If the process is not broken—improve it." – W. Edward Denning

"Doing the same thing over and over and expecting different results is the definition of insanity." – Anonymous

2013 GRADUATION RATES

- The U.S. average for 4-year public colleges is 33.3% in 4 years and 57.6% in 6 years.
- The U.S. average for 4-year private colleges is 52.8% in 4 years and 65.4% in 6 years.

SITUATION ANALYSIS

- Average student loan debt approaches $30,000. About 70% of 2013 graduates left college with an average of $29,400 in debt.
  Source: Institutes for College Access and Success
- We know that people with college degrees earn significantly more money than those without degrees. As many people—perhaps more—who have student loan debts, also have college degrees.
- This debt is causing financial stress in students and families. Some are questioning the value of college degrees and many students feel unprepared and pessimistic about their future financial and career success.
- 17 states pledge to increase graduation rates joining a New National Effort. "We all acknowledge that the objective of access to higher education is not first entry, it is completion."

Source: Copyright @ 2016 The Chronicle of Higher Education

NEW COLLEGE DEGREES IN HAND: NOW WHAT?

A focus of the study was the underemployment of recent college graduates. The underemployment rate for new college graduates has risen substantially with a growing number of graduates accepting jobs that are part-time or low paying jobs or both. Steadily rising, the underemployment rate for recent graduates increases from 34 percent in 2001 to 44 percent by 2012. The data for 2014 still shows that recent graduates are having a hard time finding good jobs.

Source: March 2014 Monthly Labor Census: U.S. Bureau of Labor Statistics

This is the first generation (millennium) that most young people feel that they will not be as successful as their parents were in their careers.

We do not want our young people or older ones losing Hope for the future. Is it any wonder that people feel that we should be doing something different and more effective with retention and graduation rates?

Basically, what our text does is:

1. Give direction for career choices, particularly in situations like the following:
   - "I don't know what to do."
   - "I don't know what I'm cut out to do."
   - "I don't know what choices I have."
2. Simplify the job search process by giving a step-by-step process.
3. Encourage students to learn their "Core Competencies" or strengths, and what value they bring to the job.
4. Teach students how to use social media to discover the needs, goals, and strategies of the companies with which they want to work.
5. Help students gain hope, as well as confidence in themselves and the future.

LEARNING OUTCOME

Describe the measurable skills, abilities, knowledge, or value that students / job seekers should be able to do or demonstrate as a result of this text.

Outcomes

- I have a step-by-step job search process.
- I know what motivates me personally and professionally in order to know the type of jobs or careers that are the best fit for me.
- I have a list of accomplishments that confirm my strengths and provide me with the confidence to communicate them to others.
- I fully understand how to develop a resume, stressing my strengths and skills.
- I have confirmed my strengths to myself and am able to effectively communicate them for the job I desire.
- I see my role as a "salesperson" and this is necessary for a change in the paradigm and shift to a new game, a new set of rules for getting a job and starting a career.
- I will decide if I'm going to develop digital and/or printed portfolios.
- I will have joined LinkenIn and learn how to maximize its benefits.
- I realize the importance of being a referral in my job search.
- I have developed my networking target list.
- I know the value of informational interviewing and how to utilize them.
- I fully understand the potential of the "hidden" job market and how to access it.
- I fully understand the potential of social media and how to use it to help me get the job I want.

If you know what you want, expect to get it, have done enough for the other person, ask for what you want, and follow a definite plan, you will get what you want.

Overview of the 12 levels of the Pathway to Success

Getting the Right Job:

A Personal Guide to Developing Your Career

If you know what you want, have done enough for the other person, expect to get it, follow a definite plan, you will get what you want.

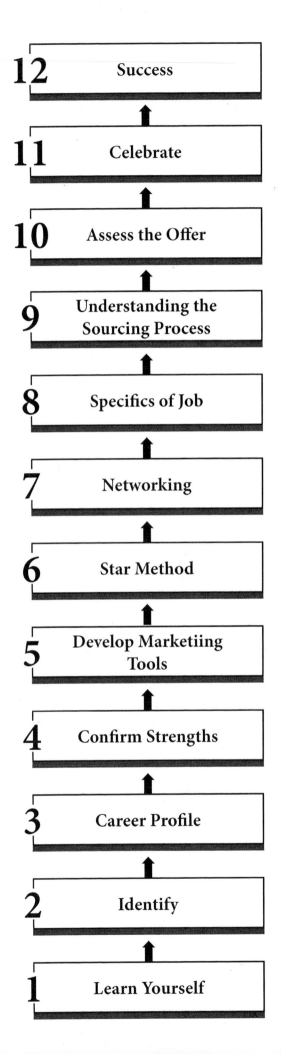

12	Success
11	Celebrate
10	Assess the Offer
9	Understanding the Sourcing Process
8	Specifics of Job
7	Networking
6	Star Method
5	Develop Marketiing Tools
4	Confirm Strengths
3	Career Profile
2	Identify
1	Learn Yourself

Pathway
Getting the Right Job to Develop Your Career

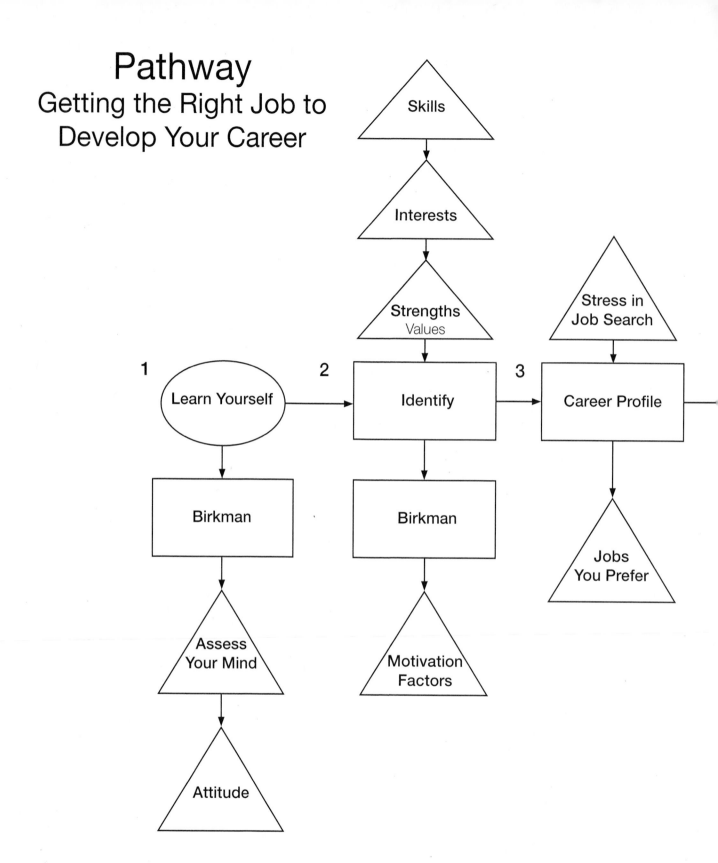

Skills

Interests

Strengths
Values

Stress in
Job Search

1

Learn Yourself

2

Identify

3

Career Profile

Birkman

Birkman

Jobs
You Prefer

Assess
Your Mind

Motivation
Factors

Attitude

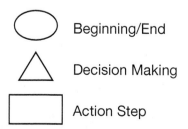

Beginning/End

Decision Making

Action Step

x

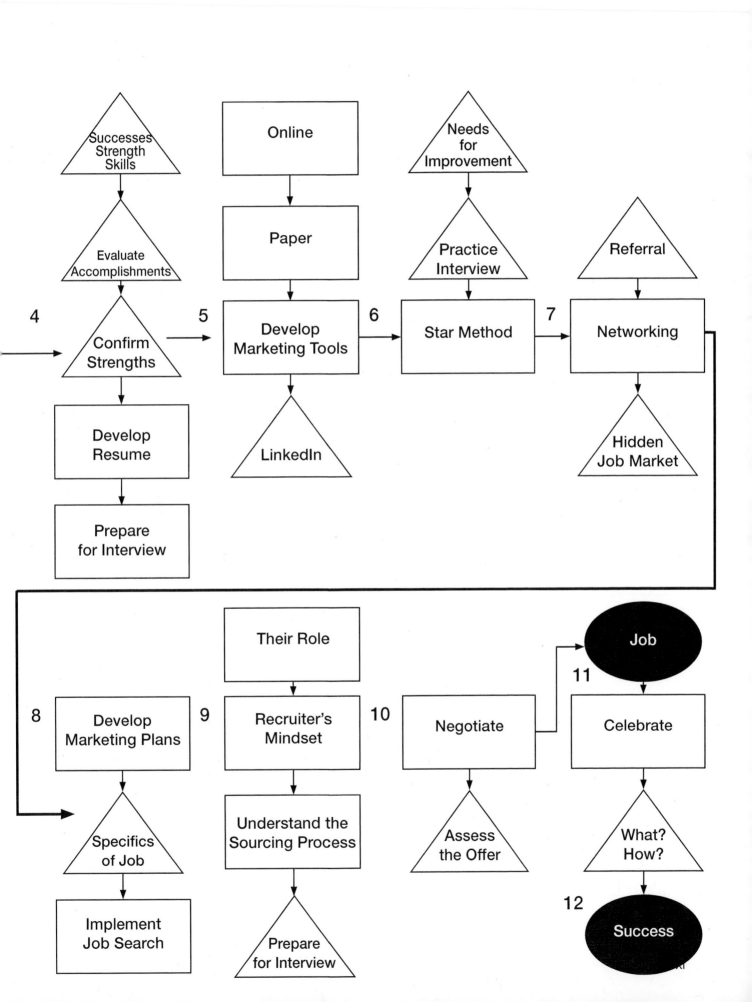

INTRODUCTION

Learning and following the process as outlined in this book will ensure that you will be prepared, competitive, determined, and confident as you seek employment and the best job for you. To get the most out of this book, you should read each Birkman Method® report as referenced throughout the book, and you should complete the exercises scattered throughout each chapter.

This will allow you to realize the following outcomes:

- Using the Birkman Method®, you will fine-tune your plan and skills in light of your personal strengths and interests.

- You will be prepared and motivated to spend the necessary time to find the right job-fit for you.

- You will be confident and knowledgeable about the interviewing procedures you will face.

- The right job will enable you to be successful and move up to the next level of your personal development.

Expectancies

A hallmark of this book will be nurturing the spirit. Spirit involves energy, enthusiasm, desire, and commitment. It is what moves us. Together we will create an environment that is supportive of learning, encourages risk taking, develops empowerment, and does not punish failure. We need to feel safe in learning by trial and error. We learn far more from our mistakes than from our success.

Fun and celebration will be a vital part of the recognition and praise you will give yourself for progress. This will spur continuous improvement and provide you support and encouragement.

It will also be necessary for you to foster and embrace change. The easiest path for each of us to take is our current course. It may not be the most effective course, but we are familiar with it and know its limitations and problems. If we stick with it, we will avoid further troubles; we will also never see further improvements. Searching for a better way to do things brings new wishes and unforeseen problems, but it also brings new benefits and rewards.

> ### *Nuggets of Wisdom:*
>
> - We are all given a part of the universe to transform and improve – ourselves. The best mind to have is an open mind.
>
> - Learn what it is you need to know.
>
> - Believe in miracles.
>
> - Entertain new ideas.
>
> - Keep building self-confidence.
>
> - Learn, Learn, and Learn.

HOW TO USE THIS RESOURCE

This book is designed to be used in tandem with the Birkman Method® questionnaire results. In order to complete the exercises in this workbook, you must complete the questionnaire prior toutilizing the workbook.

Steps for Getting the Most Out of This Resource

1. Locate your unique access code on the inside cover of this book complete the Birkman Method® questionnaire.

2. Set aside 30-45 minutes to complete the questionnaire. It is best if you complete the questionnaire in one sitting.

3. While answering the questions, go with your first response; don't overthink your answers.

4. Once completed, follow the instructions on the screen to download and/or print your results. You will need these to complete the exercises contained in this book.

This book and assignments require the active participation of each person. Successful job search and improvement in careers doesn't just happen—success depends on training and achievingpersonal excellence.

This creative approach or process will prove to have the highest success rate in job hunting andcareer enhancement.

TABLE OF CONTENTS

Chapter 1
Assessing Your State of Mind

Outcome:

- I will develop a new attitude toward embracing change and taking risks.

- I will know that I am creative because I can borrow materials/ideas and adapt and adopt them to achieve my goals.

DECISION

The first step in the job search process begins within one's self. You must make the decision to personally prepare for the upcoming journey by making changes that will make possible a successful job search and/or career change.

To adapt ourselves for maximum career fulfillment, we must change the way we personally approach challenges and adversity. This discussion harkens back to our fight or flight tendencies, and we all have unique combinations of tendencies and various ways of responding. Understanding these issues in light of a job search or career change is essential.

As described in the Introduction, this book will incorporate your unique Birkman Method® Results. You will be asked to refer to your results at points where understanding your unique tendencies is essential to working through the job search process. We will begin this process here based on the need for you to understand your basic tendencies and responses to changes and hardship. With that in mind, **please refer to the first report in your results packet, Topic 1, "Your Job Search" and refer to Section 2 of this report, "When the Job Search Becomes Stressful." Please read this section thoroughly before continuing.**

You can expect some or all of these emotions as you begin this journey. In view of these revelations, consider the following: an over reliance on security and the status quo is harmful for job performance. It is all too easy to do just enough to get by. Trying to implement change involves taking risks, and taking risks involves the possibility of failure. Too often, rather than risking failure we stay with old methods and practices. This is the safe route, but it also cuts off any possibility of advancement. Safety is the most unrewarding goal to work toward. It keeps us from learning new things and gets in the way of our reaching our true potential. We need a new attitude toward taking chances and making changes.

The more you push the boundaries of comfort, the more you will become able to take risks and make difficult decisions. An important part of risk taking is personal responsibility. You can't have one without the other. You can expect that some risks will pay off, but you must also expect some to fail. When you take a chance and make a mistake, be accountable for your actions. Admit you made an error, and explain why you undertook the step in the first place.

Honesty and accountability are key. But there is a payoff: even when you make mistakes, you can learn from them. You can grow.

And that's the whole point of risk taking and change: ultimately, they lead to new knowledge and personal growth. Whenever change comes your way, don't ask yourself, "What can I do to cope with this and ride it out?". Ask instead, "What can I do to embrace these challenges, to learn from them, and ultimately improve myself and advance my personal vision?".

Please be aware that you do have unique strengths and tendencies that will serve you well during the job search process. Being reminded of those now will provide a strong foundation for your next steps. With that in mind, **please refer to the first report in your results packet, Topic 1 "Your Job Search" and refer to Section 1 of this report, "Approaching Your Job Search." Please read this section thoroughly before continuing.**

Begin now considering how you will leverage these strengths to your benefit moving forward, noting that the tendencies and characteristics listed in the Birkman report just referenced are things that come naturally to you.

The business world today offers us a host of challenges that, at times, seem to bear down and smother us. If we look challenges in the eye and see them as an opportunity for growth, learning, and improvement, we will begin changing the way we view our journey.

Exercise 1

1. In light of the Birkman results shared in this section, what aspect of your personality do you believe may be your biggest obstacle in this process?

2. Similarly, what job search activities that do come naturally to you may be your biggest asset?

ATTITUDE

We need a positive attitude toward taking chances and making changes. Pushing ourselves to make difficult choices and actively seeking change will enable us to attempt activities that we are not particularly comfortable with; the more we push the boundaries of comfort, the more we become able to take risks and make difficult decisions.

Attitude isn't something imposed upon us from the outside. It's a choice. Some people respond to an uncertain business or job climate by distancing themselves from their jobs and seeking fulfillment in sources outside their work. Their heavy emotional investment may go into hobbies and other leisure-time activities, for example. But isolating our identity and sense of spiritual well-being from our work denies a crucial fact: our jobs are a vital aspect of our lives, and each day we spend an enormous amount of our time at work.

Consider these numbers. There are 168 hours in a week. If you sleep 7 hours a night, then that leaves you with 119 hours awake. Assuming you work 40 hours per week (and most people today work far more) and must spend 2 hours each day preparing for and commuting to and from work (again, a very conservative figure), then 50 hours a week—or almost half the time you are awake—is filled with your job or job-related activities. Trying to separate personal fulfillment from your work means discarding almost half of your life and categorizing it as unfulfilling.

For our lives to be full and worthwhile, we must enjoy our work, look forward to it, and draw personal satisfaction from it. To take this one step further, we not only need to draw satisfaction from our work, we need to believe that what we do effectively leverages our God-given strengths and interests. This does not mean making work the sole focus of life; becoming so involved in a career that we neglect family and friends is just as bad as viewing our job as nothing more than a source of income. What we need to achieve is a balance between our professional lives and our personal lives. We must adapt ourselves so that even in a business climate of uncertainty and instability, we can be comfortable and can excel in our jobs and our careers. Doing so requires that we change the way we think about work, and change the way we react to conditions of the workplace.

Depending on your work experiences, or those of your parents or other family members, you may have a skewed view of "work" in general. As you continue on this job search journey it will be important that you put aside pre-conceived notions of "work" in order to ascertain what direction you take in light of your strengths and interests.

Exercise 2

1. At this point in the process, with true self-reflection, describe your current attitude about the process of job search and/or career change.

CREATIVITY

cre·ate

/krē ˈāt/

verb

Merriam-Webster dictionary defines "create" as, 1. To cause to come into existence; make, originate. 2. To cause; produce; bring about.

These definitions suggest that creative thoughts have to be original, brand new, and never before tried. How many times have you heard people say when they meet a person with a talent for writing or art, "I really envy you. I wish I were creative myself." Our standard notions of creativity are very restrictive, breaking the world up into a smaller number of creative people and a vast majority of uncreative people.

Is this division really accurate, though? Certainly, few of us are ever going to try our hand at writing a novel, painting a portrait, or creating a sculpture. But this doesn't mean that we cannot be creative. Creativity is not so much a talent as a way of thinking, which is something that can be learned and expanded. It involves the willingness to experiment and make changes, a confidence in one's own skills and capabilities, and the ability to adapt useful ideas to his or her own circumstances.

Let's look a little closer at the last dictionary definition of creativity. If we accepted it literally, then we would believe that we couldn't be creative unless we were doing things and thinking thoughts that no one has ever come up with before. But there is no writer, painter, musician, or any other artist who doesn't have models and masters from whom they have learned their techniques and received inspiration. The early work of virtually every great novelist and poet is highly imitative of the writers they admire. Only as they mature and develop do they begin to develop their own style and discover their own individual material. Some forms of art, in fact, such as the collage and digitally-sampled music, involve no original material at all. The individuality of the work—indeed the creativity—exists solely in the way in which the borrowed material is arranged and adapted.

Creativity, then, is not in the ideas and techniques we use, but rather in how we use them. Anyone can learn to be creative. We must simply look for new ideas and different ways of doing things while always taking into consideration how we can adapt those ideas for our own use.

This is easier for some than it is for others. Some individuals are wired to create and enjoy change and new ways of approaching situations, others prefer the predictable, secure methods that have been utilized in the past. As you continue to explore your Birkman Method® results throughout this book you will learn more about your natural tendencies in this area, but for now, consider the following.

Too often when we are searching for new ways of doing things, we are looking for "recipes" that we can follow step-by-step without having to modify any details. That's far easier than coming up with our own plan, but it has its dangers. Consider, for example, the countless fad diets that are printed in magazines and available online. If you want to lose weight, they claim, all you have to do is follow this simple step-by-step plan. It all sounds so easy, but these diets never really seem to work. How could they? Everyone's body is different, and one person's schedule and habits are different from another's. A single diet can't work for everyone.

The same can be said for plans and methods for improving your job search process. New books, blogs, and articles are available weekly and are loaded down with charts, graphs, plans, and techniques. No person could ever hope to implement all the plans; very few of us can fully implement our individual plan.

This is by no means to say that these available resources and plans are without merit. Oftentimes they are filled with wonderful ideas, even though their schemes cannot work for us as a whole. With that in mind, it is important to approach this book with creativity, considering what the authors have to say and analyzing the ideas they are laying out. The material is adaptable and can be modified for individual needs and preferences.

Personal growth is about becoming the person we have the potential to be. A period of unemployment or time planning for a career/job change can absolutely change your life. This can be a place where gladness and hunger meet, therefore motivating you for your journey.

Exercise 3

1. What do you need to do to personally prepare yourself for the journey to come? Write down your needs and prioritize them.

2. Write your personal expectation of this book.

Nuggets of Wisdom:

- Don't try to change anybody but yourself.

- A teacher will appear when you really want to learn.

- We are all teachers to one another.

- We can all learn from one another.

- Everybody is entitled to miracles, and miracles come in all sizes.

- Be committed to excellence, high standards, and continuing improvement —all of which equals quality.

- The scientific method of learning: confrontation, search, tryout, and evaluation is a great process for development.

Chapter 2

What Motivates You in the Workplace?

Outcome:

- I will learn what motivates me personally and professionally in order to know the type of job or career and company or organization that are the best fit.

UNDERSTANDING MOTIVATION

To motivate means to provide with an incentive or motive. Why do you need to know and be able to document your motivating factors? Because according to a new study conducted by the consulting firm Towers Perrin, which surveyed almost 90,000 workers in 19 countries, only 21% of workers are "engaged" in their jobs. "Engaged" is human resources jargon for being ready to expend some extra effort at work. Engagement is the degree to which workers connect to the job or company emotionally, are aware of what they need to do to add value, and are willing to take that action.

To be engaged, you must be motivated, and motivation is typically highest when the job offers an opportunity to learn, develop new skills, and acquire and demonstrate competence. Managers cannot get us motivated to achieve! They can help us look for opportunities to achieve and they can help build an environment that is conducive to achievement, but each of us has to assume the responsibility for our own motivation. Think about your own motivating factors—what keeps you excited about achievement?

Following is a brief exercise that can help you begin to better understand your motivating factors.

Exercise

1. Select a job you believe you would like to pursue, visualize what you want to achieve with it, and try to see in your mind that success happening at a specific time and place.

2. Now, make a written list of your motivating factors by answering this question: "What made you happy and proud at the time you visualized your success?"

Most managers and companies think that money in salary and veritable pay programs are the main motivators. Once a person's basic money needs are met, then only approximately 25% of workers are motivated by money. Listed below are some possible "individual motivating factors":

- pride
- contribution to others
- potential for increased responsibilities and income
- vision
- beliefs
- personal achievement
- personal growth
- satisfaction / commitment to a good job
- recognition
- appreciation
- autonomy / self-governance / desire to make own decisions
- high personal standards
- curiosity / desire to learn
- prestige / positive attention
- power / desire to influence people

- order / desired amount of organization in daily life

- rejection / fear of rejection / fear of job loss

- aversion to anxiety and stress

- leadership

- honor / desire to behave in accordance with codes of conduct

- family / desire to spend time with family.

This, of course, is only a partial list because we are all different. Take a moment and circle the motivators listed above you believe have the most impact on your success and satisfaction. Please do this prior to reading the remainder of this chapter.

THE BIRKMAN METHOD® AND WORKPLACE MOTIVATION

When we are first born our needs are basic. We need food, protection, physical comfort, and sleep. Babies are very in tune with these needs and they vocalize loudly to ensure these needs are met. Overtime, our needs get more complicated, as does the process of getting those needs met. In addition, our family, society, and culture may have instilled in us the idea that we should not expect to get our needs met on a regular basis, or that our needs are not that important.

Earlier in this lesson we discussed your motivating factors in general terms by utilizing a visualization exercise. Now we will peel back one more layer and focus on some very individualized, personal needs.

In the context of this book, when conducting a job search or managing a career change, your needs are extremely important. It is simply not possible to manage an effective job search process without being clearly in tune with one's needs. Job satisfaction, personal fulfillment and spiritual peace all depend upon managing needs and seeking healthy ways of getting needs met on a regular basis.

At the end of the previous chapter you were asked to list and prioritize your needs. Take a moment to glance back at what you wrote. This chapter will take this process one step further. We will focus on the Birkman Method® results to come to a deeper understanding of personal needs, with a focus on work environments that are likely to meet those needs, and on the reactive behaviors that can be predicted if those needs are not met.

Please be aware up front that this is a challenging process requiring openness and self-reflection. No inward glance is easy, and this one will be more than a glance. But, please know that true success and personal growth through this process is only possible if one first attends to the "self" and truly assesses where she is in life and what matters to her at this juncture.

With that in mind, let's begin looking at some of your Birkman Method® results focusing specifically on needs. We will look specifically at needs that relate to interpersonal and communication needs, company cultural issues, management style preferences, and general needs. To get us started, we will focus on the center of our existence: our interpersonal, or relationship needs.

Interpersonal and Communication Needs

We are relational people. All of us strive for, and long for, meaningful relationships. And even though we are not necessarily looking for these types of relationships while conducting a job search, we do have to accept the fact that other people play a key role in our success or failure in this process. With this in mind, it is crucial that we understand what we inherently need from others.

As stated in the Preface of this book, the Birkman Method's basic approach centers on understanding one's needs and the needs of others. This is the bread and butter of the instrument and its effectiveness in this process. The report you will review next provides an overarching description of your interpersonal needs and communication styles, particularly from key individuals in your life.

Exercise 1

Please locate and read Topic 2, "How to Talk to Him/Her."
Do you feel the statements about your interpersonal needs are basically true?

Do you think these needs are likely to consistently be met in the job search process?

The reality is that all of our needs are rarely going to be met all of time. The job search process is no different. It will be important for you to be aware of your personal "redflags" or reactive behaviors in these situations. These behaviors manifest when the needs in these areas are not met. They are reactionary in nature but they can be controlled. You must be able to continue moving forward in your job search without getting derailed, and knowing how you are likely to react to adversity is key. Only through knowing and understanding these behaviors can you begin to control them.

Exercise 2

Please locate and read Topic 3, "How She/He Handles Other People."

Can you think of any real life examples when these behaviors interfered with your ability move forward in a situation? If so, what did you do to get past it?

You can expect these particular behaviors to appear during this process, probably more than once. Keep in mind, however, that these needs are real and matter to you. With that in mind, it will be important that you implement strategies to manage these early on in the process. Otherwise the success of your search will be impacted in a profoundly negative way.

What are some strategies that you would utilize in this process? How will you manage these feelings and reactions?

Work Environment Needs

Most people underestimate the importance of the work environment, at least early in their careers. Honestly, most focus on *what* job they want, not where they want to work. This is a crucial mistake, one that we hope you will not make in your current search. To that end, this section will focus on gaining a greater understanding of your unique needs as it relates to work environment.

When discussing work environment, it is important to separate an understanding of the physical environment from the social and corporate culture associated with a particular workplace. While the physical can be an important factor (indoor desk setting vs. outside or manufacturing environment) what tends to matter more to most people is the management style and "feel" of the workplace.

Exercise 3

Please locate and read Topic 4, "Organizational Fit" and then take a moment to reread Topic 2, "How to Talk to Him/Her." In light of the Birkman descriptors in Topic 4, please answer the following questions:

Have you ever worked in an environment that was clearly uncomfortable for you? If yes, what do you think made you uncomfortable?

Have you worked for a specific manager who did not address the basic needs described in the Topic 2 report? If so, what could that manager have done differently to better motivate you?

Most people don't leave a job, they leave a manager. In addition, most employees do not fully understand what they need from a workplace or a manager and are unable to ask for what they need. Please make sure you are familiar with what you actually need so that you can access a job opportunity and a potential boss effectively in the future.

GENERAL NEEDS

Throughout most of this book we will highlight specific Birkman results as they relate to the tactical aspects of the job search process. We believe, however, that it is imperative that you have a basic understand of your general results before we continue the discussion. With that in mind, please take some time to carefully read the following and then record your reaction in the space provided.

Exercise 4

Please locate and read report Topic 5, "Some Basic Information About You."

Do you believe that this is an accurate description of you?

Which aspects resonated the most?

To continue this train of thought, being truly open and honest with yourself, **please read Topic 6, "His/Her Challenges."**

Exercise 5

Which of the behaviors listed in Topic 6 have you seen manifest the most in your life?

Have they interfered in past situations, making you ineffective and/or uncomfortable?

Please note: It is more important now, more than ever, that you maintain an awareness of these potential street behaviors, monitor them, and avoid them whenever possible.

Nuggets of Wisdom:

- Integrity is your greatest strength.

- Don't work for money; work for the opportunity to learn and serve.

- The key to happiness is making the decision to be happy.

- One of our purposes in life is to bring out the best within ourselves and others.

- Money is very important, but work for your dreams, beliefs, values, and what you enjoy.

- We will do the things we are interested in when it's convenient, but for the things we are committed to, we will only accept results.

- In our constantly continuing improvement, we need to see work not as it is but what it could be.

Chapter 3

Perception is Reality – What is Your Personal Brand?

Outcome:

- I will become more aware of how I am perceived as well as how I perceive others.

Whether we like it or not, others' perceptions of us become their reality. There are certainly times when others' conclusions about our behavior, accomplishments, appearance, or personality seem unfair. It also may feel like there is nothing we can actively do to control or manage the thoughts of others. While this is true at times, there are steps we can each take to control what is called our "personal brand." While you are in an active job search, maintaining a vigilant awareness of this "brand" is crucial, and an active awareness should, in reality, become part of managing your career over time.

Your "brand" is driven by your behavior and reactions, your approach to problem solving, and your interactions with others. It is also important to remember that you have a "digital" brand, thanks to the numerous social media platforms available, and to the internet in general. Both aspects of your brand will be addressed in this chapter.

YOU ARE WHO YOU ARE, BUT...

We ended the previous chapter with some general information about you, along with some potential behavioral pitfalls that may impact your search. The pitfalls listed are what Birkman calls "stress behaviors." These are reactions to situations where one's needs are not met. It is extremely important that you remain aware that these behaviors may manifest, so as to avoid or at least manage them.

First, we will focus on the way you usually behave, which most people would refer to as your personality. We believe this is how you were born, and describes the basic ways you are wired. We also believe that these behaviors describe the ways you are most productive and successful. However, regardless of how "normal" your typical behaviors may feel to you, they can be misconstrued by others.

With that in mind, we will now focus on how you are perceived by others in light of and because of some of the very characteristics that make you uniquely you. Please understand that we are not proposing that anyone strive to be something they are not, or that they attempt to change their basic makeup. The purpose here is to make you aware of how some of your typical, and we might add "comfortable," behaviors are potentially viewed by others.

We will start with a look at how you are likely to "handle" other people in a work environment.

Exercise 1

Locate and read Topic 7, "Understanding the Components," Section A: Components: Usual: Comments.

Do these descriptors feel accurate to you?

If so, do you see any areas others may perceive in a negative way?

Now let's take a look at what Birkman says about the ways in which you try to influence others. Influencing others is a very important part of the job search process. Your role as the potential employee is to influence an employer to hire you. Understanding this aspect of who you are is crucial.

Exercise 2

Locate and read Topic 8, "How He/She Seeks to Influence Others." Focus on the first section only, "Effective Approach."

Do these descriptors feel accurate to you?

If so, do you see any area others, particularly a potential employer, may perceive in a negative way?

How could you adapt any of these, if needed, to better serve your purpose in the job search process?

Now that you have evaluated these areas in light of your usual, comfortable approach, it is important to look at these same 2 areas from the perspective of stress or reactive behaviors. During the job search the level of personal stress is high simply as a result of unemployment, or underemployment. It is very likely that you will revert to stress or reactive behaviors at least occasionally, which is why we introduced them at the end of Chapter 2. We will continue to revisit them throughout the book, but for now let's simply focus on these 2 areas.

Exercise 3

Please look back at Topic 8, "How He/She Seeks to Influence Others," and this time read "Less Effective Approach."

Although none of these behaviors are very positive, do they adequately describe the ways you react when feeling stressed or pressured?

If so, which specific behaviors seem the most likely to manifest in your life?

How could they negatively impact your search and potentially derail your efforts?

Exercise 3 was probably not a fun exercise, but it is necessary in order to mentally prepare for the job search process. Please remember that in your search, and ultimately on the job, you are the "product" that is for sale. Your personal "brand" is impacted by all of your behaviors—the good and the bad. If you are going to be deliberate in managing your personal brand, then you must be aware of who you really are.

YOUR ONLINE BRAND

In discussing your personal brand it is important for you to understand that during a job search process, you are the "product" being sold. Like any product, your brand is a huge differentiator, and likely the reason you would get a job instead of someone else even when both of you have all of the same qualifications. Strong brands not only drive choice, but also value, meaning that a strong personal brand could also lead to higher pay. All the more reason to be mindful of your brand!

So, how does social media affect your personal brand? As it does with most things, social media multiplies the size and scope of your brand. If previously you were worried about what you said to someone, how you acted during an interview, or how you dressed/presented yourself in a more social occasion, consider now the amount of information potentially available about you on-line. Consider your status updates and pictures on Facebook, Tweets to friends, books and topics you noted as interesting, etc. Consider information that you make available about yourself, as well as the things your friends make available. There is a potentially enormous amount of information impacting your brand, most of it related to things that would never come up in a professional/interview setting.

It is true that there is an ongoing discussion about the ethics of firms using this personal information in hiring decisions, but there are largely no laws describing what can and cannot be used, only guidelines. Additionally, remember that recruiters are humans too, and are doing their best to find the best person for the job; it can be difficult to avoid looking up your candidates online. In fact, more than 60 percent of companies check their candidates' online profiles, and this number is likely to continue growing. So, the best approach is to actively manage what others can see about you. You will have a "digital footprint" simply by virtue of existing and interacting online, so you might as well make it work for you.

Some things that are not discussed in applications or interviews will be obvious from your digital presence: gender, race, ethnicity, age, any disabilities, etc. Now, as you know, these items are legally protected, and are not to influence hiring decisions. However, other items have cost applicants their job opportunities: inappropriate photographs, bad attitudes towards previous employers and fellow employees, discriminatory comments, or general information about drug use/abuse and or excessive alcohol use. It is also not uncommon for recruiters to gauge applicants' communication skills by how they express themselves online, nor is it unlikely for them to confirm prior experience and/or qualifications through social media. Even if many of these items are not officially entered into the firm's decision criteria, there is still the "I can't un-see this picture, or that comment" which could damage your brand, and with it your chances at landing a specific job. It is possible for recruiters to simply assume that you are "not a good fit for the company's culture" and dismiss an application at that point.

However, there is a fairly straightforward solution. Start by making your social media accounts private (if able), thus limiting what information is visible outside of your group of friends/family. Additionally, manage your list of friends carefully. Privacy settings are of little use to you if you add the recruiter/interviewer to your friends list after your meeting. At no point can recruiters request your social media passwords (this is one instance where several states have passed a law protecting individuals against social media intrusion).

For those services where privacy is not an option, consider managing your content. Pay attention to what you say, what you post, and what others post about you. This is a tremendously important step as we move away from a "hiding the bad/inappropriate stuff" strategy to using social media to your advantage as a brand-building tool. How?

Make sure that the information you are providing in your public social media accounts is consistent with what you present in person, and that both of these are consistent with the professional brand/impression you are attempting to create. This is easily done via:

1. **Engaging in online conversation.** There are several groups online that are specific for industry-related or trade-related discussions. Join the conversation to demonstrate knowledge, expertise, and interest.

2. **Sharing Content.** Engage with experts in your field and share what they have to say with others. Share interesting/relevant articles.

3. **Creating Content.** Contribute your own insights via blog posts, articles, etc.

Perception is truly reality, and social media does provide you with tools to manage perception, your image, your personal brand, and your value to potential employers. Creating a strong brand as suggested above might not only assist with current job applications, but might also translate into new opportunities as more managers and recruiters come across your content.

Nuggets of Wisdom:

- Judgment will be one of your worst enemies.

- Stay open-minded. Strive to grow in this area because generating ideas and being flexible are essential to success.

- Demonstrate respect for everybody you come in contact with and those you don't see.

- Make mistakes. Learn from them and admit to them early.

- Don't be sarcastic.

- Be honest.

- Be generous with kindness.

Chapter 4
Career Direction

Outcome:

- I will become more knowledgeable of the different careers that are out there and the ones that I am best suited for.

Many factors impact career direction. One of these factors is the power of family influence. It is no secret that parents begin prepping their children early for certain jobs and careers, either based on family history or on what the parents hope for their children. Some parents deeply desire their children to follow in their footsteps regardless of whether or not there is actual ability or interest in that specific career path. Others desperately want their children to achieve higher levels of professional success than they did, which often leads to pushing their children through school and beyond.

Many children grow into adulthood believing their future is pre-determined, and that their input and personal goals are irrelevant. Others rebel against those pressures and lose the desire to strive for any professional goals. In the end, though, the only person who truly suffers from either type of apathy is the individual themselves. If you fall into either category, now is the time to decide that it is in your best interest to become engaged in the process and spend some time determining what you really want to do.

Another factor that clearly impacts career direction is the level of opportunity for relevant education and training. Let's face it. Some people are born with access to more opportunities than others. This may begin early with the selection of a preschool or daycare. Then it may depend on where the family lives and the quality of schools for which they are zoned. For others it may be the simple need to enter the workforce early in life in order to assist with the family bills.

There are certainly times when these factors are beyond one's control, but in most cases there are ways to access the training and education needed for a specific career path. As with family pressures, it is important for an individual to understand that they do have some control over their situation and it is in their best interest to exercise that control. Determining the actual career direction, however, requires an inward look that is possible for all.

The Birkman Method® provides a great roadmap for individuals seeking to learn more about what interests them in ways that could lead to a satisfying, rewarding career. You are encouraged to spend ample time understanding your individual Birkman Career Report. This will be pivotal as you begin to see which directions may make the most sense for you. The exercises at the end of this lesson will guide you in this process.

When you completed the Birkman Assessment, you participated in an "interest" inventory where you were asked to select your preferences from a series of listed professions. The following career categories, and your respective scores, were derived from that portion of the assessment.

Please note a few things as you review this information:

1. This is NOT a measurement of skill.

2. It is a measure of interest. When given choices between specific careers, you were assessed on which professions you regularly selected and which ones you never selected.

3. Any area scored 7-10 are areas you gravitate towards and find interesting and appealing.

4. Any areas scored 4-6 are areas for which you are indifferent, meaning you don't gravitate towards or away from them.

5. Any areas scored 1-3 are areas you genuinely gravitate away from, so it is very unlikely that you would find job satisfaction or a good fit in these areas.

YOUR BIRKMAN CAREER FOCUS REPORT

Please find and read Topic 9, "Career Focus." This report is comprehensive and will take time to fully absorb. Don't rush through this reading.

Exercise 1:

Spend a few minutes rereading the areas where you scored 7-9. In the space below brainstorm the various jobs that could fall into these areas. After you have created the list, place a check mark next to the jobs that sound the most appealing.

Exercise 2:

Review the jobs you marked with a check mark in the previous exercise. Take a few minutes to rank these from "most desirable" to "least desirable" in the space provided below.

Exercise 3:

Finally, reread those areas in your Career Focus Report where your score was 1-3. In the space below, summarize these areas. As a reminder, these are areas that you typically gravitate away from, so it is important to be familiar with them as a reminder of what might be a bad career choice for you.

Nuggets of Wisdom:

- Be at least 70 to 80 percent sure that you want the job.

- The best new employees will be recommended by the present workforce. Get someone's support.

- Decide what you really want to do and be persistent. "Hang in there."

- To help decide what you really want to do, figure out your strengths and the skills you enjoy using. Determine where you would want to live your dream, who you would want to do it with, and then go for it.

- Building a dream is so much more fun and rewarding than just having a dream.

- I would rather have a dream and do nothing about it than not to have a dream at all.

- Take your foot off first base. What's the worst that can happen? Go for it!

Chapter 5

Evaluating Your Accomplishments

Outcome:

- I will recognize how much I have to offer to the world, my workplace, and the future I want to create.

- My values and principles will help to build my strength of character, which then will enhance my self-esteem and self-worth.

- I will have a list of my accomplishments that focus on my strengths and thus confirm my strengths and provide the confidence to communicate them to others.

At this point in our process you should have a better understanding of the following:

- Aspects of the job search that could derail you

- The motivating factors that must be met in your life

- The basic career direction that makes the most sense for you

Now it is time to begin personalizing your actual search.

In light of the fact that employers are primarily interested in how you can add value to their organization, you must become comfortable discussing your successes, strengths, and skillsets. Why? Because these same employers are going to evaluate you by assessing how you have added value in the past.

The first thing you must do is evaluate your past successes and consider them in light of outcomes and skills. To do this, you must begin a deep evaluation of your strengths and how those strengths have had a positive impact in the past.

In addition, please be aware that there are specific strengths and abilities for which most organizations screen. These are often referred to as core competencies. You must be able to give evidence that you possess these skills and strengths if you are going to be successful in the job search.

With this in mind, and in light of the career direction information you discovered in the previous chapter, it is time to define your strengths and skills. It is also time to clearly outline what you enjoy doing, determine where you want to use those strengths and skills, and with whom you would most want to work.

IDENTIFYING AND CONFIRMING STRENGTHS

The following is an exercise designed to acquaint you with the core competencies today's employers often screen for. This exercise is also designed to help identify specific examples from your past where your strengths and skills added value to an organization or group. To get the most from this, consider where you were when you were the happiest and working or striving to achieve certain goals or handling specific responsibilities. This could have been in school, while working part-time or full-time, or as part of a personal project, family activity, or any group or team memberships. There may be other possibilities beyond this list. Just describe and document your experiences.

Please note: It is imperative that you complete this exercise as it lays the groundwork for building all of your marketing materials and for adequate preparation for future interviews. This will take time and it may be advisable to complete the exercise in two or three sittings.

The following steps should be followed for each of the Competencies listed:

1. Examine the definition or explanation of the strength and get a feel for what it means.

2. Answer each question posed to achieve a realistic self-assessment. Please write all of your responses down in a notebook. You will need these notes in the following lesson when you begin developing your resume. This information will also be helpful later when you begin preparations for the interview process.

3. Describe in detail your past behavior that will confirm and document each competency.

Teamwork – Working effectively with others to accomplish goals

1. Describe a situation when you were an effective team member.

   a. How did you help the team?

   b. What were the results?

3. What were some of the best ideas you presented to help improve team effectiveness?

   a. What approach did you use to present these ideas?

   b. What were the results?

3. Describe a situation in school or work in which you helped another person.

   a. How did you help?

   b. What were the results?

4. Describe how you have helped a team or work group clarify roles and responsibilities.

   a. What did you do?

   b. What were the results?

5. How were goals established for your team or work group?

   a. What was your input?

   b. What were the results?

Desire to Learn – Learning and applying new information to a job or task

1. What was the most difficult task you had to learn in school?

   a. How did you go about it?

   b. What were the results?

2. What was the most difficult task you had to learn at your present job? Past jobs?

   a. How did you go about learning it?

   b. What were the results?

3. What on-the-job training or special courses have you had?

   a. How did you acquire and apply this new knowledge?

   b. What were the results?

4. Describe your process for or method of learning new information.

    a. How have you used this process or method?

    b. What were the results?

5. What awards or certificates have you received?

Initiative – Self-starting; taking action on one's own to achieve goals beyond what was expected

1. What projects have you started on your own?

    a. What was your motivation for this project?

    b. What were the results?

2. Describe a situation in which you had to take action on your own to achieve goals or perform a difficult task.

    a. What action did you take?

    b. What were the results?

3. What has been one of your most challenging responsibilities?

    a. What did you do differently than others?

    b. What were the results?

4. Describe a situation where you had to respond quickly and put in extra effort to solve a problem.

    a. What action did you take? When?

    b. What were the results?

5. Do you have any other examples or proof of your being proactive?

Honesty – Honesty / Integrity / Truthfulness: marked by being upright, fair, and truthful

1. Describe a situation where you were asked to do something that was against your morals.

    a. How did you handle the situation?

    b. What were the results?

2. In a work situation or in school, have you ever seen another person do something that you thought was unfair or dishonest?

   a. How did you feel and what did you do?

   b. What were the results?

3. Sometimes it's difficult to follow all the rules or policies and get the necessary results. Have you had to bend any rules?

   a. Describe the situation and what action you took.

   b. What were the results?

4. Describe a situation that would prove your honesty in work, school, or how you manage your life and responsibilities.

   a. What was your motivation or reason for doing the right thing at the right time?

   b. What were the results?

5. Was there a time when you were less than straightforward or truthful?

   a. What was the reason for your mistake or omission?

   b. What were the results?

Work Ethic – Doing more than expected for an average performance in a job or a situation; having high standards of performance

1. In your present position, how do you define doing a good job?

   a. How do you know you are doing a good job?

   b. What are the results of doing a good job?

2. Describe a situation where your performance exceeded others' expectations. Work? School? Hobbies?

   a. Why were your standards higher than normal?

   b. What were the results?

3. When have you been the most pleased with your performance?

   a. What did you do? What action did you take?

   b. What were the results?

4. When in school and work, what was your attendance record?

   a. What contributed to your performance?

   b. What were the results?

5. What other documentation or proof do you have to show high work ethic?

    a. What responsibilities have you handled the best?

    b. What were the results?

Persuasive / Sales Ability – To cause someone to do something by reasoning, to make someone believe something

1. Describe a time when you persuaded someone to do something that was different or difficult for them.

    a. What did you do?

    b. What were the results?

2. What knowledge do you need about someone or the situation when attempting to change their mind?

    a. When have you been successful?

    b. What were the results?

3. When have you given what you consider to be a sales presentation to someone or a group?

    a. How did you prepare?

    b. What were the results?

4. Have you been able to gain someone's support of an idea of yours?

    a. How did you do it?

    b. What were the results?

5. When have you required others' help to achieve certain goals?

    a. How did you get their help?

    b. What were the results?

Building Rapport / Developing Relationship of Mutual Trust

1. When have you developed rapport with someone that you didn't know at first?

    a. What did you do?

    b. What were the results?

2. Describe a situation where you have been involved with building an ongoing relationship.

    a. What steps have you taken to build trust?

    b. What have been the results?

3. What do you think it takes to build rapport with someone or a group?

    a. Describe a situation where you have used these skills.

    b. What were the results?

4. Describe a situation where someone was indifferent to you in the beginning of your relationship.

    a. What did you do to help bring them around?

    b. What were the results?

5. In your past jobs, how did you build rapport with your boss, co-workers, or other people?

    a. What did you do?

    b. What were the results?

Creativity / Innovation: the ability to adapt useful ideas to your own circumstances; using new ideas and different ways of doing things to achieve goals

1. Describe a situation where you used a different or new way of solving a problem.

    a. What approach did you use?

    b. What were the results?

2. When have you achieved a difficult goal using a new or different idea?

    a. What were your ideas and how did they help?

    b. What were the results?

3. Describe a situation when your methods or ways of doing something were different from other people doing the same work.

    a. How were your methods unique?

    b. What were the results?

4. What kinds of problems have people recently called on you to solve?

    a. What were your contributions to solving these problems?

    b. What were the results?

5. Describe a situation where you combined others' ideas or other resources to improve your performance or effectiveness.

   a. What were the ideas?

   b. What were the results?

Problem Solving: identifying problems, gathering information, considering possible causes, developing and prioritizing courses of action

1. What are the toughest problems you have had to solve?

   a. What did you do to identify the real problem?

   b. What were the results?

2. When have you anticipated a problem before you had to actually face it?

   a. What was the problem and when did you anticipate it?

   b. What were the results?

3. What are some problems you have had in a work situation recently?

   a. How did you solve them?

   b. What were the results?

4. Describe a situation when you have developed a process (a series of actions or functions) to improve how work is completed.

   a. What was the process?

   b. What were the results?

5. Describe a situation where a problem was best left alone and it was better to do nothing to solve it.

   a. What was the problem?

   b. What were the results?

Oral Communication: ability to express ideas clearly and concisely; to express oneself in such a way that is readily and clearly understood

1. Describe a work-related situation where it has been important for you to be clearly understood.

   a. What have you done to make sure that you are understood?

   b. What were the results?

2. What tools or techniques have you used to assure that your oral communications are understood?

   a. How did you use these?

   b. What were the results?

3. Describe any presentations you have made to a group (three people or more).

   a. What approach did you use to get your idea across?

   b. What were the results?

4. Describe a situation where it was very important for you to clearly understand another person.

   a. What did you do to ensure that you understood the other person?

   b. What were the results?

5. Describe a situation where you were a part of the audience listening to a speaker about a subject important to you.

   a. What did you do to assure that you were getting the understanding that you needed?

   b. What were the results?

Written Communications: expressing yourself clearly in writing that is adjusted to the needs and interests of the other person or audience

1. Describe the types of memos or letters you have written.

   a. What are some examples?

   b. What were the results?

2. Describe any forms you have been required to create or complete.

   a. What are some examples?

   b. What were the results?

3. Describe other written requirements you have completed.

   a. What are some examples?

   b. What were the results?

4. Describe any proposals, procedures, or reports you have written.

   a. What are some examples?

   b. What were the results?

5. How would you rate your performance in this area? What criteria is this rating based upon?

Computer Proficiency: having the ability to use software packages

1. Describe the software packages you currently use.

    a. How have you used these?

    b. What were the results?

2. Describe the areas in which you are proficient.

    a. In what areas are you most proficient?

    b. In what areas are you least proficient?

3. Describe how you have used Microsoft Word.

    a. What are some examples of letters or other documents you have created using Word?

    b. What were the results?

4. Describe your experience using email in work-related situations.

    a. For what purposes have you used email in these situations?

    b. What were the results?

5. How would you rate your performance in this area? What is your rating based upon?

Flexibility: the ability to effectively change or respond to different situations or circumstances

1. Describe a situation where you maintained effectiveness with different environments, tasks, and people.

    a. How did you maintain effectiveness?

    b. What were the results?

2. Describe a situation where you worked with people from different backgrounds or cultures.

    a. How did you work in these situations?

    b. What were the results?

3. Changing positions or assignments can be difficult.

    a. What steps or process did you use to feel comfortable and effective doing the new work?

    b. What were the results?

4. Describe how long it took you to learn the new task and responsibilities.

    a. Why did it take this amount of time?

    b. What were the results?

Job Desire: the degree to which the work itself will match with the strengths and motivation of the individual.

1. Describe your extra activities or efforts.

   a. How do these further demonstrate your ability to perform the job?

   b. How will you use these to obtain the job?

2. Describe why you want this particular job.

   a. What are the elements you like about it?

   b. Do your values match?

3. Describe your strengths and any special knowledge or skills you have.

   a. In what ways are these important?

   b. How can you put these to work for the needs and goals of the organization?

4. Describe what you think could distinguish you from other applicants.

   a. What are some of your unique qualities and experiences?

   b. What have been some notable results of your work?

5. Describe your salary requirements.

   a. Can the organization afford you?

   b. Will the pay range match up with your needs and motivation?

Visionary: characterized by vision or foresight, being able to see a desired future, and seeing how things can be different and better

1. Describe the future you picture for yourself.

   a. What does it look like?

   b. How will you achieve it?

2. Describe a personal, non-business example of when it was necessary for you to have a clear picture of what you wanted to create.

   a. How did you create that picture?

   b. How did you use it?

3. Describe a time when you stopped daily activities, goals, and challenges, and took a broad outlook toward the future.

   a. How did you make the time?

   b. What were the results?

4. Describe some of the most challenging directions/assignments you have had to implement.

   a. What steps or process did you follow to implement them?

   b. What were the results?

5. What rating would you apply to this strength? What is your rating based upon?

Planning and Organization: effective time-management, scheduling, goal-setting, and achievement

1. Describe your use of time management.

   a. What types of scheduling and other strategies have you utilized?

   b. What were the results?

2. Describe a situation at work where you had several things to do at the same time.

   a. What did you do?

   b. What were the results?

3. Describe a non-business situation where you established goals on your own initiative.

   a. What steps or process did you use?

   b. What were the results?

4. Describe a business situation where you established goals on your own initiative.

   a. What steps or process did you use?

   b. What were the results?

5. How would you rate your performance in this area? What is your rating based upon?

Ability to Handle Stress: being able to perform a job under pressure to achieve objectives within time goals

1. Describe a situation in your jobs that has been most stressful for you.

   a. What did you do?

   b. What were the results?

2. Describe when you've started a new job with little time to learn the necessary tasks.

   a. What did you do?

   b. What were the results?

3. Describe a time when you were faced with an ethical conflict in your job.

   a. What did you do?

   b. What were the results?

4. Describe how much time your present job requires you to spend away from home.

   a. How have you handled this?

   b. What have been the results?

5. How would you rate your ability to handle stress? What is your rating based upon?

Tenacity: holding firm to one's beliefs and plans to achieve goals

1. Describe some situations where you were persistent.

   a. What did you do?

   b. What were the results?

2. Describe how long it took you to complete high school or earn a college degree.

   a. What affected this amount of time?

   b. What were the results?

3. Describe some of the biggest challenges you have had to overcome to get where you are today.

   a. How did you handle them?

   b. What were the results?

4. Describe what has been your biggest personal loss.

   a. What did you do to overcome it—if you have?

   b. What were the results?

5. At some point in the careers of most of us we wonder whether we are in the best field for us. Describe a time when you have experienced this and why.

   a. What did you do?

   b. What were the results?

Energy: the capacity for action or accomplishment

1. Describe a time when you had to work for a long period of time at a fast pace.

   a. How did you handle it?

   b. What were the results?

2. Describe the amount of physical effort you put into your work in a typical day.

3. Describe a time you've worked evenings or weekends for long periods of time.

   a. How did you handle this?

   b. What were the results?

4. Describe when you usually complete your reports and paperwork.

   a. How much time does it take?

   b. What are the results?

5. How would you rate your sustaining long hours to accomplish your goals? What is your rating based upon?

Customer Orientation: listening and understanding the customer (internal and external); identifying customer's needs; giving high priority to customer satisfaction (internal and external)

1. Describe how much customer interaction you have in your present job.

   a. What percentage of your time do you spend with customers?

   b. What are the results?

2. Describe which skills are important for dealing effectively with customers.

   a. What is an example of when you've displayed those skills?

   b. What were the results?

3. Describe how you assure customers are satisfied.

   a. What steps or process do you use?

   b. What are the results?

4. Describe a time when you had to "go the extra mile" to satisfy a customer.

   a. What did you do?

   b. What were the results?

5. How do you know that you are meeting or exceeding a customer's expectations? Can you give an example?

As a closing exercise, please do the following:

1. Prioritize or rank each strength.

2. List your top five strengths and rank them 1 thru 5 in order of importance to you in light of your potential career paths.

    a. _____

    b. _____

    c. _____

    d. _____

    e. _____

Nuggets of Wisdom:

- You will know your strengths and be able to document them and therefore better communicate what you have to offer. We underestimate what we have.

- Develop your character by examining the values you believe in and practice.

- Develop the skill of visualization: the ability to see the end result.

- Remember that you have everything you need. Maybe not what you want, but what you need is already yours.

- You are already perfect; you don't need any more classes, seminars, books, or whatever to make you happy and have inner peace.

- One of your strengths is your ability to change your thoughts.

- Take good care of your mind, body, and spirit.

Chapter 6
Creating your Marketing Materials
(print and electronic)

Outcome:

- I will fully understand how to create a resume stressing my strengths and skills. I have previously confirmed my strengths to myself and will be able to effectively communicate them to the job requirements that I desire.

- I see my role as a "salesperson," and this is necessary for a change in the paradigm and shift to a new game, a new set of rules for getting a job and starting a career.

The dictionary defines "resume" as: a summary, especially a brief record of one's personal history and experience submitted with a job application. In reality, a resume's purpose is to get an interview, ideally for a desired job or position that will play to one's strengths and motivational factors.

This is a paradigm (an example or model) shift for most people, and it impacts all aspects of the search. It requires a new idea of what it takes to be successful in our job search and career.

In today's marketplace, a resume is a sale's tool. It can and should aid you in achieving what you want by landing you relevant interviews and networking opportunities. It helps you communicate in a clearer, concise, and believable manner. Oftentimes, you also will be able to demonstrate that you are aware of some of the needs and goals of the organization where you are applying for employment. This is particularly true whenever you have conducted an informational interview and a thorough search of the organization.

With all of that in mind, let's begin the process of developing a resume, designed specifically as a sales tool.

DEVELOPING YOUR RESUME

- Consider the following BEFORE starting to work on your resume.

- Write down your thoughts in the same notebook you used to record your competency based accomplishments. All of the information you have recorded will be used to build your resume.

Select an Area of Focus

Decide what type of job you want and write it at the top of a piece of paper. Think about specific job titles as well as a general career direction. Refer back to your Career Report if needed to come up with specific titles.

Education

List your educational qualifications. Include your bachelor's degree in this list and the date of your anticipated graduation.

List your total grade point averages if 3.0 or higher, or you can indicate only your major grade point average if it is 3.0 or higher.

Record any special projects or studies in which you may have taken part, such as field work, research projects, etc.

Past Work Experience

Think back through every job you have held (volunteer or paid) and detail job duties and responsibilities for each one. Try to summarize your role in two to three sentences. Write down specifics about the organization and operation including size of organization, how many employees, etc. in this section.

Accomplishments

Now, think about specific accomplishments you achieved in each job. What did you do beyond the daily expectations of the job? Refer to the notes you took in the previous lesson to remind you of specific experiences that corresponded to the core competencies outlined.

- Did you exceed sales quotas or performance goals?
- Did you save the organization money?
- Did you generate revenue?
- Did you increase efficiency or productivity?
- Did you deliver outstanding customer service?

Try to write down at least two accomplishments for each job that you can quantify or qualify in some way (see examples below). Please note these tips as you craft these statements.

- Accomplishment statements should provide evidence of your productivity and show how you added value to an organization. They briefly capture the actions you took and the results you achieved. Work to make each statement interesting so that people who read your resume will want to get more details about your accomplishments. Be sure you note any cost savings, and mention innovations, changes, or actions that show you actively produced desired results.

- Accomplishment statements should quickly communicate to employers that you can do the job. Be sure your strengths and skills come across and that everything you write down supports the job you're targeting and the strengths and skills it requires.

- If you can't answer the question "So what?" about each bullet point (meaning why/how did this action bring value to an employer?), it should be reworked to answer that question, or it should be eliminated.

Examples of Accomplishment Statements:

Strong Examples

- Introduced a continuous improvement program that minimized waste and boosted efficiency.
- Contributed to team initiatives that increased daily productivity and reduced errors.
- Increased revenue by designing eye-catching displays and utilizing suggestive selling techniques.
- Saved 10% over previous cost for part by researching prices on the internet.
- Organized a chapter of 150 women for the recruitment of over 700 potential new members.
- Planned and implemented a thrift sale, raising over $3000 for Juvenile Diabetes.
- Documented daily water safety records accurately 100% of the time.
- Created and managed daily rotation for seven lifeguards to maintain safety for swimmers.

Poor Examples

- Responsibilities included implementation of policies and procedures. Trained new employees, interfaced with subordinates and vendors and light correspondence.
- Responsible for cleaning and straightening up clothes racks at closing time.
- Dealt with customer service issues. Various sales activities.
- Assisted the public with their questions and concerns.

Community Activities

Write down any of your activities that were not associated with attendance at a school. Examples would include scouting, fundraisers, civic activities, community-sponsored athletic programs, etc. Again, think not just in terms of membership, but rather the roles you played and the accomplishments you achieved.

Example:

Organized a car wash that raised over $2000 for the community food bank.

Leadership Activities

Write down any and all activities in which you participated. For example, if you are in a fraternity or an honorary organization and you have held a leadership position, make certain that you write down your role(s) in addition to your membership(s). Describe what you did in each membership/role.

Honors and Awards

List honors and awards you have received including scholarships, athletic awards, academic awards, etc. Describe the reasons you received each honor or award.

GENERAL GUIDELINES

Before you begin the draft process, please read the following caveats, warnings, and snippets of advice from various professionals and employers. Please keep these in mind as you create your first draft.

Begin each sentence with strong action verbs like planned, organized, and directed. Make sentences positive, brief, and accurate.
Misspelled or misused words reveal careless work habits and laziness. Double and triple check every time you revise your document! Do the final check on a hard copy and not on the computer.
Employers want specifics on what you can do for them, NOT information about what you want from the job.
Everywhere and always, if you describe the duties you perform and don't include your accomplishments, your resume is virtually assured of a near-death experience.
A resume isn't your biography. Employers want to know "what have you done lately?" In other words, what have you done while in college and maybe in high school.

Wherever possible, use buzz-words relevant to the job you are seeking.
Your resume should be one page. Since some employers scan resumes looking for key phrases, make certain that you do your research and include phrases appropriate to the type of work you are seeking.
Do not use personal pronouns.
Do not use abbreviations. The only exceptions are state abbreviations and USA.
Do not use periods in abbreviations. (Wrong: U.S.A. Correct: USA)
Write out all numbers up to and including nine. Use numerals for 10 to 999,999 (except at the beginning of a sentence).

The sample on page 48 is an example of a resume that focuses on accomplishments and can therefore be customized to specific jobs or organizations. It is the preferred format, but additional samples are provided as well.

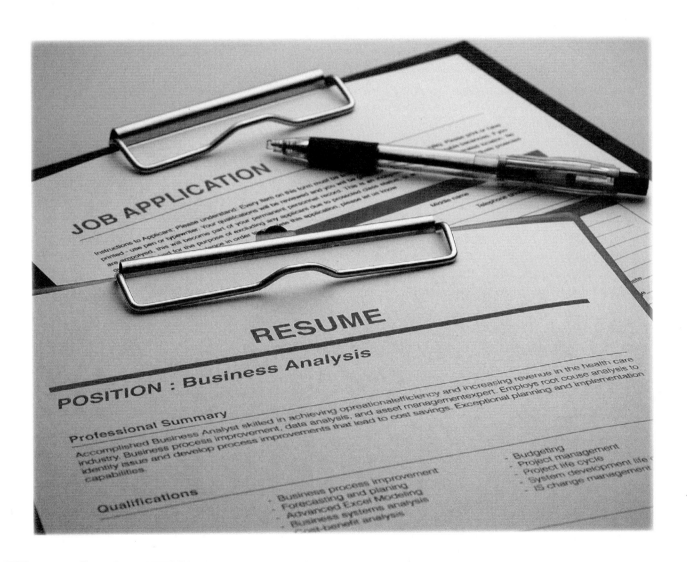

First Name and Last Name
Address Telephone Email Address

OBJECTIVE

Are you seeking an internship, full-time job, admission into grad school? Make sure the reader knows what you want to do next. Be concise with a one sentence description of your goal (Examples: Seeking an internship in sports management. Seeking a full-time position as a registered nurse in a hospital setting. Seeking admission into an MBA program.

EDUCATION

College of University, City, SC
Bachelors Degree, Month and Year you graduated (will graduate)
Major:
GPA: If over 3.0

EXPERIENCE

INSERT COMPANY'S NAME (ALL CAPS not bolded), City, State and Country
Title of the position (bold)   Month year – Month year
- Insert your accomplishment statements (2 to 4). Keep to 1 line (concise, clear, direct).
- Begin each statement with a strong action verb and end each statement with a period.
- Each should highlight an achievement and/or value-adding experience, quantified.
- Accomplishment statements should be relevant to the job you are targeting.

INSERT COMPANY'S NAME (ALL CAPS not bolded), City, State and Country
- **Title of the position (bold)**Month year – Month year
- Insert your accomplishment statements (2 to 4). Keep to 1 line (concise, clear, direct).
- Begin each statement with a strong action verb and end each statement with a period.
- Each should highlight an achievement and/or value-adding experience, quantified.

INSERT COMPANY'S NAME (ALL CAPS not bolded), City, State and Country
Title of the position (bold)   Month year – Month year
- Insert your accomplishment statements (2 to 4). Keep to 1 line (concise, clear, direct).
- Begin each statement with a strong action verb and end each statement with a period.
- Each should highlight an achievement and/or value-adding experience, quantified.

LEADERSHIP ACTIVITIES
- Insert any leadership positions you have held on or off campus if relevant (clubs, teams, church, etc.).

COMMUNITY ACTIVITIES
- Insert any community service projects, volunteer work, etc. here.

TECHNICAL SKILLS
- If you have unique technical skills, insert them here. Microsoft and internet proficiency is assumed. Only list unique programs or systems you are proficient in.

HONORS & AWARDS
- Insert your non-academic and academic awards and honors.

Marketing Focused Resume Sample

FIRSTNAME LASTNAME

Phone: +1 (555) 444-4444 | E-Mail: name@email.sc.edu | www.LinkedIn.com/in/FirstnameLastname

EDUCATION

University of South Carolina | Darla Moore School of Business   Columbia, SC USA   May 2016
  Majors: Marketing and Management   **GPA**: 3.56
  Minor: French

Institute for American Universities | The Aix Center Aix-en-Provence, France   January – May 2011
  Studied: Intercultural Management, Globalization, Professional French, Art

HONORS/AWARDS

USC's Outstanding Woman of the Year finalist, Emerging Leader, Who's Who of USC Students, Marketing Scholar

INTERNSHIP EXPERIENCE

Communications and Brands Intern | ABC Firm   Greenville, SC USA   June – August 2013
  - Conducted in-depth research and produced plan to leverage social media for recruiting.
  - Strategized to provide necessary items for over 3,000 press members for the 2012 Detroit Auto Show.
  - Facilitated the distribution of 6,000 email-based surveys for the career management team; addressed concerns and questions in a timely manner.

PROFESSIONAL EXPERIENCE

Marketing Agent | ABC Supermarket   Columbia, SC USA   January 2015 – Present
  - Led team of 10 Marketing Scholars in designing plan to build brand equity and generate exposure within targeted niche market for nationwide organic supermarket.
  - Conducted extensive research on target markets and managed peers throughout brainstorming and plan development to facilitate an effective marketing plan.

Consultant | ABC Company, INC.   Columbia, SC USA   August – December 2014
  - Co-led student team in creating a comprehensive export plan and international market entry strategy for a Spartanburg, SC company.
  - Analyzed and researched Greenfield multinational business opportunities and distilled complex data into actionable solutions in accordance with client needs and opportunities.
  - Designed complete marketing strategy to yield results in new industries in the UAE and Mexico as well as in the US domestic markets which included strategies for buying and procurement with the government.

Resident Mentor | USC University Housing   Columbia, SC USA   August 2013 – May 2014
  - Managed and supervised a university residence hall floor of 36 ethnically-diverse first-year students.
  - Worked cohesively on building a staff of 30 fellow Resident Mentors.
  - Enforced University rules to result in a safe and orderly environment as well as developed mediation and conflict resolution skills.

Team Leader | Principles of Management Class   Columbia, SC USA   January – May 2013
  - Led a team of 25 peers in the research, crafting, and presentation of a cohesive business plan to a local start-up.
  - Designed plans for finance/investment, operations, full-scale marketing as well as community and social media strategies resulting in continued success in the community.

LEADERSHIP EXPERIENCE

Vice President of Professional Development | Alpha Kappa Psi, Professional Business Fraternity   August 2015 – Present
  - Envisioned, planned, and implemented 10 events that developed personal and professional success for 125 members, chapter, and the University.
  - Pioneered and directed first ever student-led consulting team to provide philanthropic solutions to local programs and firms in the community.

International Business Advisory Council Representative | Darla Moore School of Business   August – December 2014
- Elected to work with peers to improve the function of the nation's top International Business Program.

Secretary of Student Services | Executive Cabinet of USC Student Body President   August 2013 – May 2014
- Led successful efforts to advocate the inclusion of off-campus dining services in conjunction with current Carolina Card offerings.

LANGUAGE   FRENCH   Oral | Advanced   Reading | Intermediate   Writing | Intermediate

IT SKILLS   Adobe Photoshop, Illustrator, Bridge, InDesign, Paramount Acceptance

ACTIVITIES   American Marketing Association, Carolina Finance and Investment Association, Buddies Beyond Borders, USC Dance Marathon (2014), French Club

INTERESTS   Inbound Marketing, Graphic Design

JOHN N. DOE

1313 Cocky Street, Anywhere, SC 12345 • Cell Phone (444) 555-5555

jdoe@email.sc.edu • www.linkedin.com/in/johnndoe

EDUCATION

University of South Carolina   Columbia, SC

Bachelor of Science: Finance, Darla Moore School of Business   May 2016

Minor: Spanish

Cumulative GPA: 3.5/4.0

Darla Moore School of Business Study Abroad   Monterrey, Nuevo Leon, MEXICO

Instituto Technologico de Estudios Superiores   May 2015

PROFESSIONAL EXPERIENCE

Cocky Mortgage Corporation   Columbia, SC

Search Advertising Intern   August 2014 – Present

- Analyze digital data pertaining to search queries and keywords by identifying patterns and monitoring performance to increase search results by 15%.
- Review online advertising campaigns to maximize and increase web traffic and lead-ins.
- Create ad copy and keyword research that has generated a 10% increase in company conversion rates.
- Provide evaluation reports to management that increase financial statement accuracy for accounts worth over $15 million.

Cocky Bank   Charlotte, NC

Commercial Banking Intern   May 2014 – August 2014

- Developed financial models to structure and optimize transactions with commercial clients.
- Conducted analyses on client capital structure and prepared presentations for financing proposals and new business development.
- Assisted managers with portfolio management, business development and financial analysis for the upcoming fiscal year.

LEADERSHIP EXPERIENCE

Anglers at USC, University of South Carolina   Columbia, SC

Treasurer   August 2014 – Present

- Oversee an $8,000 budget while monitoring programming, social, and meeting expenditures.
- Coordinate fundraising strategies that successfully raised $2,500 for club activities in 2015.

Alpha Kappa Psi, Beta Upsilon Chapter   Columbia, SC

Vice President of Membership   January 2014 – May 2014

- Organized recruitment and selection activities that resulted in a 20% increase in pledge class enrollment from the previous year.
- Coordinated bi-weekly pledge class events for 35 participants that included leading weekly meetings, organizing pledge class events, and conducting formal ceremonies.

RELEVANT SKILLS AND ACTIVITIES

- Habitat for Humanity, Boys & Girls Club, USC Dance Marathon
- Proficiency in Microsoft Office, Dreamweaver, Java, and HTML
- Languages: Spanish (proficient), Chinese (intermediate)

JANE DOE
1314 Cocky Street, Anywhere, SC 12345
janedoe@email.sc.edu | Skype: yourskype | U.S. Mobile: +1 (555) 444-4444

EDUCATION
UNIVERSITY OF SOUTH CAROLINA   Columbia SC
MOORE SCHOOL OF BUSINESS, **Bachelor of Science Business Administration**   Month Year – Month Year
Triple Major: Economics, Finance, Risk Management and Insurance
Minor: Spanish
GPA: 3.85 as of Month Year (specify "as of" until your final GPA, after you graduate)
Awards: Deans List, Scholarships, Awards
Honor Societies:
Activities: PricewaterhouseCoopers Tax Competition, Vanguard Externship, USC Intramurals, Track and Field Team
Courses: Introduction to Finance, Corporate Financial Analysis, Corporate Risk Management, Investment Analysis and Portfolio Management, Management of Risk and Insurance, Financial Accounting, Calculus, Statistics, Fixed Income Securities, Derivatives
Professional Associations: Carolina Finance and Investment Association,
Gamma Iota Sigma, Lambda Chapter - Carolina's International Risk Management, Insurance and Actuarial Science Society
Other memberships: *Fi Fi Fo* fraternity-sorority

OVERSEAS UNIVERSITY   City, COUNTRY
Study abroad. Classes included … , including company visits to ....   Month Year – Month Year

QUINNIPIAC UNIVERSITY, **Global Asset Management Education (G.A.M.E.) Forum**   New York, NY
Selected to be a USC Representative to the annual financial education conference   Month Year
• Participated in workshops on … and …
• Networked with Wall Street professionals and gained financial and career insights throughout the conference.

WALL STREET PREP Seminars on **Financial Statement, Valuation and DCF Modeling** using Excel October 2014
WALL STREET PREP Seminars on **M&A and LBO Financial Modeling** using Excel   January 2015

FINANCE EXPERIENCE
CITIGROUP YIELD BOOK – MOORE SCHOOL BUSINESS PARTNERSHIP   Columbia, SC
Yield Book Finance Intern, 20+ hours per week   Month Year – present
• Bullets with more specific information

INSURANCE COMPANY   City, ST
Finance and Risk Management Intern   May – August Year
Scope of work
• Bullets with more specific information indicating achievements

CAROLINA INVESTMENT ASSOCIATION   Columbia SC
Associate for the …industry sector, student-managed mock portfolio   Month Year – Month Year
Led a team of analysts and generated investment ideas for the Carolina Fund stock portfolio.
• Bullets with more specific information and performance '

LEADERSHIP EXPERIENCE
STUDENT GOVERNMENT, University of South Carolina   Columbia, SC
Title, about ? hours per week   Month Year – present

RUSSELL HOUSE UNIVERSITY UNION, University of South Carolina   Columbia, SC
Student Leader and Information Center Attendant, about ? hours per week   Month Year – present

COCKY'S READING EXPRESS ™   Month Year – present
Statewide Literacy Volunteer, 5+ hours per week. Promote literacy awareness to grades 4K-2, traveling with University Mascot Cocky, in a collaboration between USC Student Government and the School of Library and Information Science

IT SKILLS	MS Office:Excel (macros, modeling, pivot tables, Solver), Word, PowerPoint, Outlook
	RMI-Finance:@Risk, Bloomberg, Yield Book, Capital IQ, Thompson ONE, PrivCo, Gartner, LexisNexis, Hoover's
LANGUAGES	ENGLISH: Native SPANISH: Intermediate proficiency FRENCH: Basic proficiency
ACTIVITIES	Reading, skiing, golfing
	International travel includes a high school semester exchange in Lyons, FRANCE
VOLUNTEER	weekend volunteer at …

PORTFOLIO—YES OR NO?

Should you develop a digital and physical portfolio? Absolutely! Having both a physical and digital portfolio can be a great benefit, especially if your search targets are varied. To be competitive in today's marketplace, it is becoming more and more essential to represent your work and talents in this way.

A digital portfolio can complement a physical portfolio. Both are developed after your resume is completed and they are simply another way to confirm your strengths and values. They do not include or replace your resume. They provide employers additional information about you and your work, and it is becoming more and more common for employers to make final hiring decisions based on these portfolios.

The physical portfolio is a great "leave behind" after an interview and may help keep you "top of mind" after you leave. They can provide you with that needed edge showing how much you want the job.

If you decide to create either a physical or digital portfolio, consider the following:

- Use a graphic designer and print shop, and remember to listen to their recommendations.
- Be concise. Show 15-20 pieces that will prove you are qualified for the job.
- Study the company's website to learn about the company and what strengths/values they are expecting in candidates.
- Tailor the portfolio to the job and the company's needs.
- Have a portfolio that can be easily edited for other companies and jobs.
- Place the best and most relevant work first and finish with strong pieces that reflect your strengths and values.
- Include a variety of examples of work you have done. These can be from school, internships, part-time jobs, hobbies, and community activities.
- You can use a sequence of photos, spreadsheets, graphs, and anything else that shows your thought process, development of ideas, analytical thinking, creativity, and innovation.
- Know your portfolio and how to use it in an interview to sell yourself.

Nuggets of Wisdom

- Everything in the universe is structured to grow. You can change without growing, but you cannot grow without changing.

- Write out a vision statement for yourself.

- Learn what it is you need to know.

- Use your resume as a sales aid.

- Plan a great presentation on yourself.

- Have a desk and office area for work at home.

- Be sincere and believable.

- Figure out what motivates you, besides money.

- Learn to laugh at yourself.

Chapter 7
Preparing for a Successful Interview

Outcomes:

- I know what will be expected of me in the interview process. I have confidence in myself because of my ability to prove my strengths and skills. I know how to make the interviewer's job easier.

BIRKMAN AND THE INTERVIEW PROCESS

Being interviewed by strangers who hold your fate in their hands is typically an unpleasant and unnerving experience. Some of us are naturally more comfortable in this arena, while others would rather face just about anything else other than that first handshake and the all-important prompt to "Tell me about yourself."

Understanding your natural proclivities in this area is crucial as you continue the preparation process, anticipating your upcoming interviews. With that in mind, we will again look to your Birkman results to learn more about the best ways you can prepare for this inevitable part of the job search process.

Let's start by looking at the ways in which you are at your best in an interview.

Please locate and read Topic 10, "How He/She Approaches Job Interviews, SECTION A: When He/She is at His/Her Best in the Interview."

Exercise 1

Do you tend to agree with most of the statements in Topic 10, Section A? Yes/No

Did you answer "no"? If so, your next step is to show this list to someone in your life who is close to you and ask them if they agree or disagree with these statements. If they agree with these statements and you do not, it is likely that you are currently viewing yourself in a negative light, probably due to the current state of your employment.

Take this as an opportunity to celebrate your natural strengths in this area, even if you feel quite removed from them at the moment. As your confidence returns, you will likely embrace these characteristics and use them to your advantage. It will be important that you experience an attitude shift in this area prior to an actual interview if these strengths are to be leveraged. This is something only you can accomplish, and it may require a great deal of soul searching. If you need help with that process, please seek professional guidance from a licensed therapist as a part of your job search process.

Once you are feeling more in-tune with these strengths please proceed to the next section and complete the associated exercises.

Exercise 2

1. Think back through previous interviews and recall a time when these characteristics clearly played to your advantage. Record that memory in the space provided below.

2. Has there been a time in your past when you performed badly in an interview and these strengths did not play to your advantage? If so, record that memory in the space provided below.

3. If you answered "yes" to previous question, please spend a few minutes contemplating what influences contributed to your lack of success in that situation and record your thoughts in the space provided below.

Various factors contribute to unsuccessful interviews. For now, however, we will focus on the factors that tie directly to the Birkman and the "needs" we have been discussing since Chapter 1.

Please locate and read Topic 10, "How He/She Approaches Job Interviews, Section B: When He/She is Less at Ease in an Interview."

Now, look back at your answer to #3 in Exercise 2. Do any of these Birkman statements coincide with your thoughts as to why you were unsuccessful in a previous interview? In other words, did these behaviors manifest in previous situations?

These are real risks for you in an interview setting. These are, as you probably assumed, the stress behaviors that may rear their ugly head when you are in the pressure cooker that can be an interview.

Birkman provides a few suggestions for how to prepare for, and hopefully avoid, these potential stress reactions. **Please locate and read Topic 10, "How He/She Approaches Job Interviews, Section C: Preparing for an Interview."**

The only aspect of an interview you can actually control is your preparation and reactions. You cannot control the interviewer, which is why it is crucial that you be aware of your tendencies and work hard to control them and prepare for situations that could potentially trigger them.

UNDERSTANDING THE LAY OF THE LAND

Understanding yourself and the ways in which you might respond in the process is only a part of understanding the interview itself. You also must understand the other player(s) in the process, the interviewer(s).

The Various Roles of the Players — You and Them

Good or bad, most interviewers make up their minds about the applicant in the first five minutes. The rest of the time is spent confirming their opinion, whether it is positive or negative. As they do this through questioning, which will be discussed a little later, they will also be gathering necessary information to fill out forms that are required by their company. These forms contain the questions they are to ask, along with a place for them to record your answers. Also, there will most likely be an Applicant Evaluation Form for the Personal Interview. This form is where the interviewer(s) record their reactions and opinions of you. These forms are required by Human Resources to assure that all applicants are treated the same.

With this in mind, please understand your actual role in the process, as well as that of the interviewer(s).

Your role is to build credibility with the interviewer, sell yourself, make the job of decision making easier for the interviewer, and get the job or a promise for the second interview. In most situations, the first interviewer does not make the final decision. They will re-interview or turn you down, or refer to another manager. In some very rare cases, they can make a job offer. Regardless, you must get a commitment for another interview or negotiate time to consider an offer if it is made.

Please remember the person sitting in front of you has the power or influence to hire and wants to know the following things about you:

- Why are you interviewing with this potential employer?
- What can you do for them? (your strengths and skills for their needs and goals)
- What kind of person are you? (character, strengths, skills, and special knowledge)
- What distinguishes you from other people/applicants?
- Can they afford you?

You, as the applicant need to ask the same questions in a different form:

- What does the job involve?
- How do my strengths, skills, and motivational factors match the job?
- Does this corporate culture, and the do the people who work here, meet my needs as discussed earlier in this book?
- What can I do to convince them of my strengths and uniqueness, differentiating me from others?
- What can I do to convince them to hire me at the salary I need or want?

In addition, the role of the interviewer is to gather the necessary information to make a documented recommendation to their boss and/or human resources. They may require two or three interviews – make their job easier by keeping in mind the paperwork that will be required of them. An example of an evaluation form will require they fill out the following information:

- source of referral
- position applied for
- strengths with regard to meeting job needs (they will refer to written Principal Qualifications and Duties/Job Descriptions)
- shortcomings with regard to meeting job needs (make sure any weaknesses that you describe in the interview are not important to the job needs)

- overall evaluation of applicant (summary of strengths and shortcomings as they affect their decision)

- an explanation of disposition of applicant.

Keeping all of this in mind, you must be prepared, in advance, to share the top 3-4 things you believe this interviewer/employer should know about you. This should be based on a clear understanding of your strengths and accomplishments as discussed in the previous chapters. You should be able to elaborate on all of your strengths and accomplishments, so you must be strategic and select those that are most relevant to this particular situation.

Before each interview you should spend significant time researching the company and studying the job description (read more about this in Chapter 13) in order to determine the most important things you want them to know about you. This means, of course, that you must be fully versed in your own strengths and accomplishments and prepared to talk about them in meaningful ways.

What is a Behavioral Interview?

Many interviewers will use what is known as a Behavioral Interview. This type of interview is based on the premise that past behavior is the best predictor of future performance. The following are true of this type of interview.

- Questions are developed around the traits and skills they deem necessary for succeeding in the position, organization, or field.

- These questions require you to give evidence of your skills, experience, and personal qualities, not just list them.

- You must develop a list of experiences that cover the skills and characteristics required for the position. Your work on defining your accomplishments earlier in the book will be the foundation for preparing for these types of interviews. Have your notes from Chapter 5 close by.

The following are some examples of often-used behavioral-based interviewing prompts and questions:

➢ Describe a situation where you had to accomplish an independent project.

➢ Tell me about a time that you were a member of a team. What was your role? What did the team accomplish?

➢ Describe a business situation which created stress for you.

➢ Give me an example of a situation where you had conflict with another employee in a work situation. How did you handle it?

➢ Give me an example of a project you completed successfully.

➢ What is your leadership style? Give me an example of a situation where you exhibited leadership.

➢ Give me an example of a situation where you made an improvement in your prior business situation.

➢ Give me an example of one of your personal goals. How do you plan to achieve that goal?

➢ Give me an example of a situation where you had to work under pressure.

➢ Describe a situation where you managed people to accomplish a task.

In order to prepare for this type of interview you must be very prepared to talk about what you have accomplished in the past. The best way to do this is to follow what is known in the human resources field as the STAR method. In a nutshell, this technique is designed to see if you are a good fit for their job. Your job is to prove that you are by highlighting your past successes in a succinct and relevant way. Here is how it works.

stands for Situation
Your Job: Explain, briefly, the background and the situation you found yourself in.

stands for Task
Your Job: Explain, specifically, what you had to accomplish, overcome, or solve.

stands for Actions
Your Job: Explain, specifically, what you did and why you did what you did to accomplish what you accomplished.

stands for Results
Your Job: Quantify and/or qualify the results of your actions. Did you solve it? Did it save or make money? Did it improve a process, a relationship, etc.? How did you ADD VALUE?

Exercise

With the STAR method in mind, look back at Chapter 3 and select an accomplishment that you highlighted during those exercises. Use the following template to craft a story explaining the accomplishment you selected, transforming the explanation into a STAR interview answer.

S – Situation: Briefly describe the situation and setting for your listener.

T – Task: Explain, specifically, what you had to accomplish, overcome, or solve.

A – Actions: Explain, specifically, what you did and why you did what you did.

R – Results: Quantify and/or qualify the results of your actions. Did you solve it? Did it save or make money? Did it improve a process, a relationship, etc.? How did you ADD VALUE?

Skill/Strengths: Finally, list what skills and strengths you utilized in this situation.

Now for the Heavy Lifting

Although you did much of the heavy lifting in Chapter 3 as you thought through your accomplishments, in order for that work to actually help you in the interview, you must do the following:

Exercise

Use the STAR template on the previous page to craft STAR statements for each of the accomplishments discussed in Chapter 3. This will be tedious and time consuming, but if this work is done well, the interview will go well. This may be the most important exercise in this book, so please take it seriously.

INTERVIEW DOS AND DON'TS

Regardless of interview type or the experience level of the person conducting the interview, there are some universal "truths" you need to know.

Listed below are some of the obvious **Dos**:

1. Wear business attire for all interviews, which means: wear a suit! This means that the jacket and the pants match. For men, a tie, shoes, and a belt should match. Ladies, pantsuits are usually fine, and if you do wear a skirt make sure it is at least knee-length.

2. Maintain eye contact.

3. Assure that you have a firm handshake – you want to achieve impact from your appearance and confidence.

4. Listen to the questions and take time to make sure you understand the question before formulating your response.

5. Be clear and concise when you ask your planned questions – jot down the answers and make notes during the interview. This shows interest in the other person and gives you time to pause and think.

Don'ts:

1. It is NEVER appropriate to take a call, read a text, or check social media in an interview. NEVER! Leave your cell phone in the car.

2. Don't let the interviewer control the entire interview by taking all of the time with their questions. Remember that you should be prepared with 3-4 things you need them to know about you. Make sure you share that information.

3. Don't interrupt them, but make sure you have enough control to achieve what you need to accomplish.

Questions to Consider BEFORE the Interview

The following questions are ones you are likely to encounter, thus you should prepare for them beforehand in order to be successful in your answers.

1. Tell me about yourself.
   - Some interviewers ask this to simply break the ice. Others ask to see what you view as important. And, others ask it to see if you will share something they can't legally ask.

- Your job is to prepare a 1-2 minute "elevator speech" for use when answering this question. This should focus on your strengths and skills and include basic information about the 3-4 things you want them to know about you. This is your chance to set the stage. You should not include personal information in this response.

2. Why are you here? Why do you want to work with us?

   - This gives you the opportunity to demonstrate what you have learned about the company and your initiative in developing your individual marketing plan. We will talk more about company research later in Chapter 14.

3. What distinguishes you from other applicants?

   - Relate your strengths, skills, and motivating factors to the assumed needs and goals of the company. This relates back to the work you did in chapters 4 and 5. You must be completely aware of and comfortable discussing your strengths and accomplishments.

4. What kind of salary/income are you expecting?

   - Answer with a question, i.e., "What is the salary range for this position?" If there is no range or they are not saying, respond with: "I think a position like this would be in the range of $." Have a specific amount that you want to start at with the opportunity to increase with a Pay for Performance increase in the near future.

5. What do you want or expect in a job?

   - Opportunity to perform – be rewarded – be recognized – and advance in responsibilities only after establishing a positive track record.

6. How long would it take for you to be a top performer?

   - "Could you give me a time that it has taken in the past for others, and I will beat that time by 3 to 6 months." If they don't give you a time for the average or top performers – be realistic and say six months to one year.

7. Are you willing to relocate?

   - "Yes. I would have preferences, but I would not let those get in the way of this job and opportunity." Get the job offer first and then decide if you want to relocate.

8. Where would you like to be in five years?

   - You need to seriously think about where you truly want to be in 5 years. You need to be specific enough to show you have thought about this, but general enough to ensure you don't talk yourself out of the job.

   - You could ask a question like this if you want to learn more before answering: "What is the usual next step in advancement – job position – and in what length of time on average?"

9. How long would you stay with us?

    - "As long as we both feel that I am making significant contributions to the company."

10. What is a typical day like with your present job?

    - "I'm responsible for ... and held accountable for ... ."

    - Keep your answer brief, but emphasize strengths, skills, tasks, and motivating factors.

11. Why are you leaving your present job?

    - Don't be negative and don't change answers. If you were laid off, you need to briefly explain the circumstances and then move on.

    - "I believe your company will offer more of a challenge and opportunities for personal development or growth."

12. What would an ideal working environment look like for you?

    - "Having a manager or boss who would: ... ." How you complete this sentence should be directly related to what you now know you need based on your Birkman results. BUT, always keep in mind that no boss will ever meet all of your needs.

13. How would you describe your present company? Boss?

    - Be positive. Never, NEVER say anything negative about anyone or an organization.

    - You could always answer with something simple like this: "They provided me with experience and opportunities to prove myself."

14. Have you made suggestions or ideas that were implemented by your present manager or company?

    - If they ask this, it is the perfect opening to share an accomplishment using the STAR method. This is why you decide before the interview the 3-4 things you want them to know about you.

    - Be brief, but describe in detail and share results. Refer back to your STAR stories.

15. With your present company or last position, what were three or five of your significant accomplishments?

    - You should be completely ready for this question if you did the STAR statements for all of your accomplishments. Answer completely, touching on every aspect of the STAR technique.

16. Why haven't you found a new position before now?

- If still working, emphasize time requirements of present job and limited time for search and interviewing.

  – If not presently working, share that you have been working hard to complete a full self-assessment process to ensure you find a job that is the right fit. This is in their best interest too!

17. When we do a reference check, what will they say are your greatest strengths and weaknesses?

- Keep in mind that reference checks should be referred to Human Resources and they will only confirm dates of employment.

- Answer with your strengths in different words but the same meaning.

- With weaknesses – only give ones that are not needed for the job or can be turned into attributes or positives.

18. Can you work under pressures, time goals, deadlines, etc.?

- Be completely comfortable with your Birkman strengths and share this here.

19. In your present position or recent past experiences, what problems did you identify and solve?

- This is another opportunity to use your STAR stories.

20. What other companies or type of jobs are you considering or interviewing for?

- Keep your answer related only to this company's field.

- Be honest if you are currently interviewing with other competitive companies, but you do not have to say which ones. DO say, however, if you have been invited in for other interviews and they have shown interest in you, but that you would prefer the job and company you are presently interviewing for. Be able to answer the question: "Why would you prefer us?"

TELEPHONE SCREENING

Just so you are aware, prior to the first face-to-face interview, a telephone or Skype/FaceTime screening interview may be conducted. The purpose of this is to screen applicants to decide if they warrant a face-to-face interview. If not, they will tell you they have other more qualified applicants. They will have to fill out a Telephone Interview Evaluation form. An example form will have these types of questions:

1. How did you become interested in a job with us?

2. What steps did you take to determine that I was the person to contact?

3. What is your understanding of the principal duties and qualifications of the job?

4. Please describe your current employment. If not employed, why?

5. Why do you want to leave your present position?

6. Tell me about your education:

    - degree
    - experience
    - grade point average

7. Do you have a valid driver's license?

They will have to comment on each of these questions on the Telephone Interview Evaluation form, so again make it easier for them by supplying as much documenting data as possible and by being fully prepared to answer questions about your past using the STAR method.

All of the forms that will be used, including the job application, will focus on the strengths and skills needed for the job. You have to supply the evidence that you, indeed, have the necessary strengths and skills. This evidence or documenting data helps to build credibility, assists the interviewer in filling out forms, and supplies the necessary information to make the decision – and support his/her decision to the other decision makers. Interviewers will have to justify their decision regardless of the disposition of the applicant. Make it easy for them to support you and their decision.

INTERVIEW BLUNDERS

In most any interview you are likely to blunder a question or two. That said, there are ways to recover and regain the interest of the recruiter. Here are a couple of pointers to remember if you feel the interview is not going well.

1. If you believe the interviewer has lost interest or is bored, stop talking and ask a question. This will usually inject energy into the conversation and allow the interviewer to become re-engaged in the process.

2. There will be times when you are asked a question for which you genuinely don't have an answer. This could be a behavioral question and you have not had an experience like the one referenced, or it could be a question that simply stumps you. Use the following as a guideline for tackling these tough situations:

    a. Behavioral Question: If you have truly not had an experience related to the question, skirt the time reference and talk about what you would do if you were to encounter such a situation in the future.

b. Stumped: Ask the interviewer to repeat the question, and if you still don't know how to answer, be honest and tell the interviewer that you don't know. Making something up at this point will cause more harm than good, so being honest is your best bet.

3. If you get off track and realize that you are not making sense, stop and ask the interviewer if you can start over.

FINAL THOUGHTS ON INTERVIEWING

The more time and effort you put into the exercises outlined in this chapter, and the entire book, the better prepared you will be for other questions and the interview. If, up until now, you have whizzed by the sections of this book that required you to think, work, or write, now is a good time to go back and actually complete the exercises. You won't be sorry!

Nuggets of Wisdom:

- Be positive.

- Dress appropriately for specific occasions.

- Autonomy is a much better motivator than money.

- The best mind to have is an open mind.

- Avoid pessimism and sarcasm.

- Do not bite your fingernails.

- Learn to smile easily.

- Take a public speaking course.

Chapter 8

Networking

Outcome:

- I know that networking is a crucial part of the job search process and I am prepared and ready to do it effectively. I understand I must become a referral in order to land the job I want, and I understand the important ways social media, especially LinkedIn, can impact the networking process.

The term networking at times has a negative connotation, conjuring up images of a used car salesman or that slick, slippery guy at a cocktail party. While there are folks who take the concept to the extreme, put aside your preconceived notions and consider the value of networking in securing the right job for your future. Let's discuss why networking is so important before we look to your Birkman results for some insight into how easy it may, or may not be, for you. Please take this topic very seriously, and believe us when we say that your future may depend upon it!

BECOMING A REFERRAL

Dictionary.com provides this definition of *refer*: "to direct the attention or thoughts of." It also states that a *referral* is "a person recommended to someone or for something." Thus, becoming a referral means that someone else has directed an employer's attention towards you, and they have recommended you for a job. Put that way, it should be clear why this would be a desired outcome in your search. Clearly, the best way to create a competitive advantage on your job search is to be a referral.

Hiring for any position is expensive, particularly if the wrong person is hired. For this reason, companies pay thousands of dollars to obtain job candidates from employment agencies, internet and print ads, college recruiting, and job fairs. Because of the expense of these approaches, employers are turning more and more to referrals, because they are free. They simply need someone they trust to recommend a qualified candidate.

This becomes even more important for you as the job seeker when you consider that many open jobs do not make it to the open job market because they are filled by referrals. It is estimated that 50 to 60 percent of open jobs in the private sector are filled by referrals. Now do you see why you want to be one of those referrals? So, how does this work? First and foremost, referrals are usually made by employees of companies, although they can also come from other sources like professors or customers. For this reason, it is crucial that you communicate to as many people as possible that you are in the job market. It is especially important that anyone you know working for a company you are targeting is aware of your situation.

Employees are most likely to refer people who they feel will be good performers and have a good background for their company. They generally will not refer poor performers, because that would reflect poorly on them. In addition, they will usually share information about the company and the interviewing process to the candidate which can be a huge benefit during the interview process.

Case Study Examples

Let's look at a few real life cases to emphasize why networking and referrals are so important.

> ### Actual Case 1: College Graduate Networking
>
> *A recent college graduate is seeking a job in accounting. She decides that she wants to try to become a referral. She is going to use the networking approach. First she checks with all her relatives (who work for a variety of companies). She asks for possible contacts and gives them copies of her resume. She then contacts students in her class and her professors and gives them copies of her resume and seeks company contacts front them. She contacts graduates of her school who are already out working. She also goes to her college Career Management Center, repeating the same process. Overall she has made at least 100 job-related contacts. Eventually, 2 job openings arise from this process. She receives information from the employees who referred her about the interviewing process. She interviews for both jobs and receives an offer for one of the jobs.*

It is said that the average person knows at least 250 people. If you contact 100 people, you can potentially reach 25,000; if you contact 200, you can potentially reach 50,000. Consequently, net working is clearly the best method for reaching as many people as possible, and becoming a referral as often as possible. If you are a referral, you will have some inside knowledge about the company.

An employee who can vouch for your character and potential performance will be recommending you, which means you have jumped over other candidates who are applying through traditional processes. The company will be saving money in its recruiting process and knows that the candidate comes from an employee or a trusted outside source (professor or customer).

Actual Case 2: Management Referral

A management employee of a major company has begun a job search. He contacts his friends and business associates to begin the networking process. A friend who is an employee of another major company refers him to an open job in his company. This company has a reputation for having a very difficult selection process for management candidates. The candidate gets a briefing on the interview process. The company uses a behavioral, targeted selection process (STAR method) with a series of group interviews that cover problem solving, style of management, teamwork, and technical issues. The candidate prepares for the interview process by rehearsing behavioral questions covering all of the issues. He completes the interviewing process successfully and is offered the job. Without the briefing from the friend who referred him, this interview could have been a disaster.

There are additional reasons why an employee of a company would want to refer qualified individuals to their company. Many companies are so interested in referrals that they create incentive or bonus programs to have their employees generate more referrals. They will pay cash ($500 to $1000) for each referral, or give company products or credits to buy company products. One consumer electronics company gives credits that can be used to purchase their products from inventory.

The key is that the same candidate could cost 25 percent of the salary if an employment agency places the candidate ($10,000 fee for a $40,000 job placement), or $3,000 to $6,000 for a decent print ad in major market publications or large ads in online job boards. **Consequently, the best way for a company to get candidates is through referrals, and the best way for a candidate to get to a company is by being a referral.**

Actual Case 3: The Last Candidate for a Senior Job

A major company was conducting a search for a Vice President of Operations. The search firm had presented 13 candidates, but the company was not completely satisfied with the candidates. During the same period that the search was being conducted, a vice president (VP) from another company in a similar business was given notice because her company was being sold. The VP who was given notice networked with all her resources. She had wide business connections. One of the people she networked with was a boss who knew the search firm that was handling the open job. The former boss referred her to the search firm. They interviewed her and presented her as a candidate for the open VP job.

The boss and the search firm prepped her on the interview process, and she did a comprehensive study of the company and all its businesses. Needless to say she got the job. She was the 14th and last candidate. Networking paid off for her.

HOW TO NETWORK EFFECTIVELY

Effective networking is always going to involve a conversation with another human being, so do not be fooled into thinking that you can do all of this online. **That being said, however, social media networks now play a major role in the networking process. Their purpose is to make contact with large numbers of people at once, but the end result should always be a conversation, if at all possible.**

Your online contacts from Facebook and LinkedIn, or anywhere else, could be the ones supporting your application to a new job, or the ones to let you know about a new opportunity in the first place. Having a strong network of supporters is incredibly valuable in any career, and even more so when looking for the next/best opportunity.

Managing your online network has one additional important caveat: you are not "collecting friends." Many people get lost in the numbers game, much in the same way that companies fight over who has the largest number of fans on Facebook, but you have to ask yourself this question: what is the value of adding one additional name to your contacts list if they never see/hear anything from you? It should be clear that being a silent member of your own network is not going to get you results, and that having the most number of connections is fairly meaningless compared to having a few people that are engaged with and supportive of you.

With networking, connections should be leads to future conversations. The same is true in social media, but the barriers associated with these conversations are much smaller. You should join conversations, particularly on LinkedIn, to demonstrate your interests and expertise. Engage further, share others' content, comment on it, congratulate them on achievements, etc. It does not need to be excessive, or invasive, but you should make an honest effort to enter the conversation, to remain relevant, visible, and engaged.

The key point to remember is that having lots of contacts is helpful but not sufficient for success. Your success will depend on how you use your network, and you'll need to **add** value to it by contributing conversation, content, and insight before you can **extract** value from it in the form of job opportunities and referrals. Building the network and your value to it does not happen overnight. It takes a significant amount of time and effort, but you'll be able to reap benefits from it now, and likely for a very long time afterwards.

While all social media platforms can be useful for networking, LinkedIn has emerged as the Facebook for professional networking. With LinkedIn you can develop a large number of contacts by linking electronically in your own personal network. Many people have several hundred connections through LinkedIn, and some even have over 1,000 connections. There are also many subgroups appearing on LinkedIn such as employees from a particular company or industry, and groups of alumni from specific colleges and universities. This networking process is gaining wide acceptance, and many companies are now advertising openings on LinkedIn, making it a viable resource for job search. As stated in Chapter 3, how your profiles represent you on all social media platforms is critical, but having and maintaining a living, active LinkedIn profile is essential. With that in mind, please take the time needed to complete the following exercise.

Exercise 1

You should now have a completed resume which provides the basic information needed to create your LinkedIn profile. You will also need a professional photo (headshot) for use on your LinkedIn page. Go to linkedin.com to create your page, or update it using your new resume, and start "linking" to people you know and requesting introductions to people who can possibly help you with your search!

Exercise 2

All social media platforms are now being used by employers to determine the character of a candidate and if they are a likely fit for a job. Take the time right now to thoroughly inspect your social media profiles, posts and pictures (facebook, Instagram, twitter, etc) and remove anything that might send the wrong message to an employer. Cross check your security settings as well to protect yourself from unwanted tags or associations.

NETWORKING AND YOUR BIRKMAN RESULTS

Before moving to the final assignment in this chapter, take a few minutes to review some of your Birkman results in light of the networking process, what is required to network effectively, and how both may make you feel or react.

Locate and read Topic 3, "How He/She Handles other People, Section 2: His/Her Less Effective Approach."

Exercise 3

Take a moment to re-read each of the statements in this section slowly, considering how these tendencies might impact your ability to network effectively. Record your thoughts below.

Locate and Read Topic 3, "How He/She Handles other People, Section 1: When He/She is at His/Her Best."

Exercise 4

Take a moment to consider each of the statements in context of developing a strategy for networking that will play to your strengths. In the space below write down at least 5 words that describe your networking strengths.

GETTING STARTED

Finally, this chapter will have little impact on your search if you don't start using the information immediately. Ideally you'll have a working list of 100+ networking contacts, but for now, a list of 10 will get you moving in the right direction. In the space below list 10 people you know who may have professional contacts, particularly in the companies or organizations that interest you. Once you have completed the list, follow the instructions provided at the end of the chapter to begin expanding and utilizing this network.

	Name	Company	Contact Information (email, cell)
1			
2			
3			
4			
5			
6			
7			
8			
9			
10			

WHAT'S NEXT?

To utilize this networking list effectively, do the following within the next 5 days:

1. Check to see if the contacts listed have LinkedIn accounts. If so, ask to "connect" to them.

2. Email or call them and let them know you are in the market and inform them of your specific career objective and your unique qualifications.

3. Ask them for an informational interview.

4. Email them your resume, if they ask for one.

5. Ask for additional names of individuals they know who may be able to assist you.

You are on your way! Continue these steps with every new contact and your network will grow fast. The faster it grows, the sooner you will find yourself employed and starting the career of your dreams.

Nuggets of Wisdom:

- Stay in touch with old friends and make new ones.

- Listen, listen, listen.

- Being a good listener is also being aware of the other person's mindset and not trying to change it.

- Spend some time with successful business people you know. Learn from and share thoughts with them.

- You cannot demand respect and commitment. They are only returned after you have given them to others.

- Be careful whose name you use as a reference or proof.

- Remember this wise thought: "You get what you need by giving others what they want."

- Above all, your credibility is your most important asset.

- Learn from others.

Chapter 9

Defining the Search Parameters

Outcome:

- I know what factors will drive my search, including location, function, and industry or sector.

If you have made it this far in the book, you have clearly done significant self-reflection and work towards understanding who you are, your strengths and accomplishments, and your general career direction. In addition, you now have a resume and LinkedIn profile polished and ready. Now it is time to determine what job search parameters you will set in light of the current marketplace and your unique desires and restrictions.

There are three key factors that guide the search process: location, job function, and industry. For most people, one of these factors is much more important that the other two, but for some all three are equally important. Only you can make that determination for your search, and many factors contribute to the varied weights of these factors.

If you are single, location may currently not be a factor, but it might become a major factor once you are married, cohabitating, or have children. Job function is often the main driver for those with skills-based degrees or experience, like nurses, engineers, teachers, or law enforcement officers. Others may be more open regarding what they do, but know they want to be in a specific industry (tourism, healthcare, sports and athletics, etc.). Often the industry preference is driven by what interests someone on a personal level, so be mindful of this as you work through the exercises in this chapter.

The following exercises are designed to guide you as you define and fine-tune your specific search parameters along with the associated weight of each one. Please seriously consider the questions asked, and take whatever time is necessary to provide your answers, as they will guide the rest of the search process.

Exercise 1

Location: Do you have geographical limitations, or are you free to move anywhere for the right opportunity?

_____ I am free to move anywhere

_____ I have geographical limitations

If you indicated you have limitations, please complete the following:

  I need to be within _____ miles of this location: _____

OR

I would prefer to, or need to, live in one of the following cities:

1)

2)

3)

OR

I would prefer to, or need to, live in the following regions/country/province:

Exercise 2

Job Function: Based on the work you did in Chapter 4 related to your Career Directions, what are the three to five job functions you will target? Prioritize them below with #1 being your top preference.

1.

2.

3.

4.

5.

Exercise 3

Based on all you have learned about yourself so far, what industry(ies) or business sector(s) are you most attracted to at this point (e.g., law enforcement, healthcare, K-12 education, tourism, media, agribusiness, entertainment, sports operations, etc.)? List 5 in rank order.

1.

2.

3.

4.

5.

Exercise 4

Based on your answers in the previous exercises, you have all the information needed to record your search parameters in summary form. This information will drive your research, your conversations, your networking, and your interviewing. In the space below, record your answers creating a concise Parameters Summary. You will calculate the "Importance Value" requested once this portion of the exercise is complete.

JOB SEARCH PARAMETERS SUMMARY

My primary geographic targets are _____.

(Importance _____)

My primary job function targets are _____.

(Importance _____)

My industry or business sector targets are _____.

(Importance _____)

Finally, you must determine the importance, or weight, of these factors to determine how to define and develop your marketing plan. With 100 being the total value available, please assign a value to each of the 3 factors listed above. You may divide them equally (33.3 each) or you may have 1 that is the lead driver with 80 points and the other two factor at 10 each. There is no wrong answer, but determining the right answer for you is critical.

Now you have the parameters to begin your search. In the next chapter you will use this information to develop an actual marketing plan, with a specific employer. You are well on your way to finding the job of your dreams!

Nuggets of Wisdom:

- Just say "no" to anything that compromises your values and principles.

- Our power lies in the clarity of our vision and getting others to share it.

- You will keep moving in your present direction. If you like it, speed it up. If you do not, then change it.

- Learn to love what you do by going to work each day to serve the needs of others.

- Know what you want, what you need, and learn to tell the difference.

- Remember your priorities.

Chapter 10

Developing Your Marketing Plan

Outcome:

- I now have a structured, well-thought-out marketing plan and understand my top targets and the best ways to enhance my opportunities within those organizations.

At this point, you have defined your strengths and accomplishments, you have a resume and a LinkedIn profile established, and, thanks to the Birkman Method®, you have a better understanding of how this search process is likely to impact you, and where you may struggle. Finally, you understand the importance of networking and have assessed the market and your specific search parameters. With all of that in place, it is time to begin the marketing process and get your search underway.

For this to be effective you must fully embrace the concept that "you are the product." You must approach the marketing process with this mindset. As with any marketing initiative for a specific product, this will require that you develop a plan you intend to follow. For many, this can be the hardest part of the process. It requires a systematic approach, similar to formal project management in a corporate environment. This approach is necessary because it allows you to set goals and success criteria, track your steps, and measure your progress.

DEVELOPING THE PLAN

In the previous chapter you determined the geographic parameters for your search. Please review these specifics and write them here:

- Search Locations (s): _____

- In the previous chapter you also determined what industry(s) were of most interest to you. Please list those again here:

  _____

- Finally, as a part of your work in the previous chapter, you fine-tuned the specific jobs or functions that you should target. Please list those here: _____

Exercise 1

With these specifics mind, it is time to develop a target list of 20 companies or organizations in your target location(s) that fit your industry preference(s) and have positions in line with your chosen job or function. We will refer to this as your Top 20 List. You will use Table 10.1 to keep track of your targets.

This will require research and will take some time, so do not rush the process. Take whatever time is needed to develop a relevant list from which to work. The following resources will be useful as you refine this list:

Hoovers.com

Careerinfonet.org

Glassdoor.com

Vault.com

Career-advice.monster.com

TARGET ORGANIZATIONS (TABLE 10.1)

	Industry	Location	Company/Organization
1			
2			
3			
4			
5			
6			
7			
8			
9			
10			
11			
12			
13			
14			
15			
16			
17			
18			
19			
20			

Now that you have established your Top 20 List, it is time to revisit the networking exercise on page 75. Are any of the people listed on your previous networking list employed at any of the targets you listed above? If so, list them again in Table 10.2.

NETWORKING RESOURCES (TABLE 10.2)

Networking Name	Target Company	Their Role	Contact Info

Assuming that you did not fill up the chart with networking contacts you have already identified, it is now time to expand your networking list. To do this, you will need to use your LinkedIn account, and other social media options to search for contacts within these companies and organizations. You will also need to talk to friends and family members to source additional names.

Your entire network should be aware of your target list and should assist you in adding more names to it. Also, you will continue to add to this list as you speak with people personally about your interest in their company or organization. You may choose to develop a spreadsheet for use as you continue to expand this list. Either way, please understand that this list should expand regularly as you advance through your search.

TOTAL PACKAGE

Congratulations! You have completed all of the preparation work and have compiled a Personal Marketing Plan with the following components:

- Resume
- LinkedIn Profile
- Target List
- Networking list

Now it's time to put all of this preparation to work.

Nuggets of Wisdom:

- The best investments you can make are in your career and a savings program.

- One of the best ways to solve problems is to anticipate them. What problems or opportunities will we have in six months, one year, or three years?

- Learn from your failures.

Chapter 11

Implementing Your Search

Outcome:

- I have begun an active job search using the tools, marketing materials, and lists already developed.

You've worked hard developing your marketing materials, your plan, and your networking list. Now it's time to put the plan into action. You will be implementing your plan utilizing several strategies simultaneously. These include:

1. Conducting informational interviews

2. Searching for open positions on company websites

3. Using search engines

4. Contacting employment agencies or headhunters

5. Utilizing your college or university's career center

INFORMATIONAL INTERVIEWS

One of the most important parts of the search process is arranging for informational interviews. These are conversations with individuals who have some affiliation with one of your target companies/ organizations. The purpose of these conversations **IS** NOT TO ASK FOR A JOB. It is to learn more about the industry, the company or the function within both.

This is an essential component of your search, allowing you to determine if you truly want to work for a particular employer, within a specific industry, or in certain job. The following questions are examples of things you could ask during one of these conversations.

1. Can you tell me about the advantages of working with your employer or within your industry?

2. Are there unique challenges facing your employer where my skills and experience might be of use?

3. Why did you decide to work here?

4. What attracted you to this industry?

5. What advice do you have for me as I try to gain employment here or in this industry?

6. Do you know of anyone else I should speak with to learn more as I continue my search?

Please note: You absolutely MUST ask #6. You should leave every informational interview with the name of someone else you can call to arrange another informational interview.

Why is this so important?

1. You must continue to widen your network

2. You want to be "top of mind" for a large number of people so that when they do have an opportunity available they think of you BEFORE THE JOB IS EVEN POSTED.

The more informational interviews you can schedule, the more successful your search will be. The more people you talk to, the more people know who you are and understand your career objectives. Keep calling, keep talking, and keep asking for someone else's name!

To facilitate this process, we suggest that you set "contact targets" for each week. A sample **"Contact/Application Tracking Sheet"** is provided on page 89. This tracking sheet can help you keep track of your progress. We strongly encourage you to use this sheet, or one like it, to make sure you are using your time in the most effective and efficient ways.

EMPLOYER WEBSITES

Although the process of applying for positions on a company's website can be extremely frustrating, you simply must go through the process. You must regularly search the sites of the organizations on your Top 20 List and continuously apply, formally, on the websites.

Why is this so important? In short: it's company policy. Even if you become a referral for a position that is open and posted on the company website, you are most likely not going to land an interview if you are not "in their system." With this in mind, get organized, follow a set schedule, set targets, and apply, apply, apply!

However, clicking "submit" should not be the end of the process. Crosscheck your networking list and contact anyone affiliated with the company to let them know that you have just applied for a job. They may be in a position to "put in a good word for you," or formally refer you.

When you apply for a job, the outcome you want is an interview. Work both angles, the formal process and the networking process, to better your chances of landing that interview!

Table 11.1 will help you structure your approach to this process. It also will help you track your networking contacts, as described in the previous section.

TABLE 11.1 CONTACT/APPLICATION TRACKING SHEET

	Week 1	Week 2	Week 3	Week 4	Week 5	Week 6	Week 7	Week 8
Networking Contacts Target								
Networking Contacts Made								
Informational Interview Target								
Informational Interviews Completed								
Top 20 Website Applications Target								
Top 20 Applications Completed								
Networking Contacts Informed of Applications								
Job Interviews Scheduled								
Job Interviews Completed								

SEARCH ENGINES

In recent years, many employers have begun utilizing large search engines like Monster.com and Careerbuilder.com. To hedge your search effectively, you must be engaged with these sites. Keep the following in mind as you create accounts on these engines and submit your marketing materials.

- Be vigilant about ensuring your information is up-to-date and current. You can't post a resume once and never return to update it or confirm its validity.

- Utilize the search agent options available on each site to provide notices in your email when a position is posted that fits your parameter. This "push" notification is much more efficient than manually searching the site every day.

- Focus on the companies you have listed in your Top 40 list, but be open to expanding your list if you find opportunities on these sites that interest you.

Finally, just as with the company websites, if you do find opportunities and complete applications through these sites remember to utilize your network to determine if you know someone within the organization. If so, you should contact them and let them know that you have completed an online application via this method.

Currently, the best large search engines include:

- Monster.com
- Careerbuilder.com
- Indeed.com
- Simplyhired.com
- Linkedup.com
- Employment Agencies/Headhunters

In the next chapter we will explore these options from the employer's perspective but here will provide some basic information for you, as the potential candidate.

COLLEGE OR UNIVERSITY CAREER CENTER

If you are a college student in the internship or job market you should contact your school's career center during your junior year, at the latest. They will work with you to prepare your marketing materials, assess your options, and assist you in preparing for the interview and negotiating process. What is equally as valuable, however, is the employer network available to you as a student. If you are a recent alum this is also the most valuable aspect of reconnecting with your career center.

In some sense, employers that regularly recruit at a specific school already view the candidates from that school as referrals. The programs of study and the career coaching are known entities to the recruiters and they have placed their faith in both when committing to recruit or screen resumes. They trust the school and its personnel so you would be foolish to not utilize this network.

Most likely you will be required to have a resume approved and create an account within the school's online recruiting program. This becomes another search engine for you and you should treat it as you would the large engines discussed earlier in this chapter.

Finally, utilizing your school's resources, which might include access to a LinkedIn or Facebook alumni groups, gives you access to a vital networking option: your school's alumni. Alumni are typically very receptive to assisting students from their school or fellow alumni, so don't be hesitant to ask for their help.

So now you have the materials, you are prepared to interview, you have a plan, and you know the job search processes. It's time to start your search. Get started today!

Nuggets of Wisdom:

- Think process, process, process, or system, system, system, for getting something done or for continuing improvement toward your vision.

- Learn to go from A to B to C. It's very rare for anyone to jump from A to Z.

- Momentum and progress are so important because they will keep you moving in the intended direction.

- Personal growth is about becoming the person you have the potential to be.

- Do it now.

- Do not be so hard on yourself.

- Follow up, and then more follow up.

- Plan your work. Work your plan.

- Focus on results.

Chapter 12

Understanding the Sourcing & Screening Process

Outcome:

- I more fully understand the mind of the recruiter and have additional knowledge and insight that will help me navigate the search process.

OVERVIEW

In the current economy, when turnover occurs in an organization, meaning someone has left an existing position, it is not immediately assumed that the position will be filled. Initially, the job will be assessed to determine if it can be eliminated or if the duties can be divided up among other existing positions. The target is to save money, and all companies are attempting to manage their resources in a cost effective manner. If the position survives this process, and it is determined that a hire must be made, the job description, job requirements, and compensation are evaluated to make sure that the recruiters and candidates have a clear understanding of the qualifications for the job. Once this has occurred, the recruiter can begin sourcing for the job. "Sourcing" is the human resources process of seeking qualified candidates.

Something similar happens when new work is added within an organization. New work can develop when there is an increased demand for the products or services provided by the organization, when new products or services are introduced, and/or when new technology or methods are integrated into the organization. In these cases, a similar evaluation is conducted of the duties that need to be performed. If it is determined that a new person must be hired, the human resources office will develop a job description, determine job requirements and compensation for the job, and begin sourcing for the position.

INTERNAL CANDIDATES

Typically, the company will seek internal candidates first. Most organizations have an internal job posting process, allowing interested and qualified internal candidates to bid for the open job. Qualified candidates are interviewed, with the best candidate selected to fill the opening. Considering internal candidates in this fashion creates good morale and commitment in the organization.

REFERRALS

If there are no internal candidates, the organization will look for external candidates. A company's first resource is usually their "hot file" of resumes. This file will generally consist of referrals from employees or other sources, and candidates seen for other openings that have good general experience for the organization. Many companies will electronically scan the resumes of these potential candidates into a system where they can be retrieved by entering job specifications. It is not uncommon for an organization to seek out a candidate that has been in the hot file for 6 months or more. As discussed in Chapter 8, jobs filled in this manner never get to the market (known as silent job market), and filling them is virtually free to the company.

If the hot file doesn't produce a candidate, the company will seek other types of referrals. Similar to the hot file, there is no additional cost for candidates who are referrals. Frequently, the human resources department will circulate or post a list of open jobs so current employees can generate referrals. As discussed in Chapter 8, this is why it is crucial that you constantly work your network within the organizations on your target list!

Obviously, organizations view referrals in a very favorable manner. There is very little cost associated with a referral and they generally come with a perception of a positive performance outcome (employees will not refer someone who will reflect poorly on them). Another positive aspect of sourcing referrals centers on the candidate's view of the organization. In general, the organization can assume that the referring employee has briefed the candidate about the company in a favorable fashion and provided an overview to assist the candidate in preparing for an interview.

Keep in mind that the cost of advertising open jobs, college recruiting, attending job fairs, and using employment agencies is very expensive for companies, sometimes running as high as 25 percent of the candidate's starting salary. For this reason, you can expect that seeking a referral will always be the first sourcing method used by organizations, which is why the networking process continues to be your most important line of attack in your search.

Case 1: A Significant Savings for a Company with a Referral Compared to Normal Recruiting Sources

The recruiter for a software company had the assignment to hire 3 new software engineers to help with growing volume from new customers. The average salary for the position was $110,000. The company's website was not pulling candidates. The recruiter checked the costs of recruiting sources and found that an employment agency would charge 25 percent of the starting salary, or $82,000, to fill the 3 positions. The right kinds of ads in publications and online sites would cost a minimum $20,000. He decided to post the job internally to seek referrals. He offered an incentive of $1,000 for any software engineer referred and hired, payable after the new employee completed 6 months of service. In the end, the total recruiting cost was $3,000, a substantial savings over conventional recruiting sources.

Many companies have instituted bonus or incentive programs for employees who make referrals. These incentives are usually cash, credits to buy company products, or credits to buy products from a premium catalog. Companies are also reaching out to customers, suppliers and others—trade associations, college professors, and friends. Referrals save companies large amounts of money and most of the positions filled by referrals never make appear on the open job market.

ORGANIZATION WEBSITE POSTINGS

If the referral process is unsuccessful, the most common next step is for the organization to use its website for recruiting. Next to a referral, use of the company website is the least expensive approach to recruiting and sources. Over time, company websites have become very sophisticated recruiting tools. Keep in mind that most all companies will list middle-level and lower-level openings on their websites, but they do not always list upper-level jobs.

They will generally post the open job title, a job description, the physical location of the job, and any special requirements of the job. Some employers will have a sign-in procedure for candidates to submit their resumes online and they may require the candidate to fill in a formal employment application and/or attest that their resume is factually correct (if the candidate is hired and subsequent lies are found, the candidate can be terminated). Additionally, some companies will require an online aptitude test, and possibly a brief background check to further qualify the candidate.

> ### Case 2: Partial Background Check at Time of Resume Submission
>
> *A major retail chain does a brief background check on any resume that passes their initial screening process. All candidates sign a release that permits a background check. The retail chain has major concerns with any candidate that has a conviction for a felony, or that has severe credit problems. The issue is theft. The data indicates that employee theft is on the rise, and they want to eliminate candidates that have any potential for theft. Their online application system has a direct interface with a large background checking organization, so checking these factors is a simple process. In almost all cases these types of background checks can be performed with online resources. When the background check turns up a problem, the candidate is eliminated. For successful candidates, a full background check is completed later, before an employment offer is finalized.*

COLLEGE RECRUITING

Most major organizations seek a close relationship with a few colleges or universities that produce qualified candidates for their particular business. It is also important that graduates from a particular school have proven to be successful in their organization. Often the employer will provide financial support to these schools, participate on advisory boards, and serve as guest lecturers in classes. In the past, companies would have a broader involvement with a large number of schools, but in today's economy companies want to be sure that they are getting good value for their investment. Most have decreased the numbers of schools where they recruit, seeking higher value at each, with attention paid to finding the schools with the graduate population that is the best fit for their organization. Why have businesses decreased their number of college or university relationships?

Keep in mind that sourcing through referrals and company websites costs very little and is incredibly cost effective for the organization. On the other hand, college recruiting is expensive. These costs include hiring the relevant recruiters, associated benefits and office space, equipment, travel, lodging, and the cost of meetings with students.

Many colleges have a career management office that serves as the primary interface with outside organizations interested in hiring students. These college offices will work with students to help them improve their resumes, interviewing skills, and their job search capability. Usually students upload their resumes into a system that employers can access and post open jobs. The career services office will also coordinate company recruiting on campus.

When companies prepare to recruit on campus, they can post their open jobs and review the resumes of interested students in advance. Companies will also host "open house" meetings for students. Keep in mind that every meeting between a company representative and a candidate is part of the screening process. Companies are constantly observing how a candidate handles himself, how he is dressed and groomed, and how he communicates.

Companies will use this same process when they recruit at trade or technical schools.

Case 3: Missing Out on an Opportunity

A university professor invited a guest speaker from the human resources department of a major retail organization to present the company's recruiting process to the class. The guest lecturer mentioned to the professor that she would accept resumes from the class members at the end of the lecture. The professor let the class know in advance that the company would accept resumes after the class. During the class, it was clear that the company representative was observing the class during her presentation. She was looking for class participation, engagement, and how students were dressed. At the end of the class, each student who wanted to submit a resume had a brief period of time to speak to the company representative. She evaluated how they communicated, presented their capabilities, were groomed and dressed, and what they knew about the company. After collecting a dozen resumes, the corporate representative sat down and evaluated everyone based on their skills, the brief presentation of their resumes, their participation in class, and the ways they were dressed and groomed. She stated that anytime she is involved in a class, open house, or job fair, she is always evaluating everyone she meets as a potential candidate. She added that she expected people who want to be candidates to realize that in almost every situation, she is considering anyone she meets as a potential candidate.

Generally, during the college recruiting process, recruiters typically gain only a superficial knowledge of potential candidates (unless there is time for a full interview). Consequently, the candidates that are moved along in the process are those who make a good initial impression, and not necessarily those who will be the best employees. Never underestimate the power of the first impression!

JOB FAIRS

Many colleges, universities, and outside organizations sponsor job or career fairs. A fair is an opportunity for candidates to meet numerous employers gathered in one location who are looking for job candidates and open jobs to fill. For the employer it is an opportunity to meet numerous candidates in one location, allowing them to potentially source multiple candidates at once.

Sometimes companies pay a fee to participate. This is particularly true of high tech and other occupations where candidates are scarce. Even if there is no fee for the company, there are other costs associated with a job fair. Paid staff must attend the event, which includes travel and lodging expenses, fair site expenses, and some miscellaneous expenses. The return on their investment is based on the number of people they hire from the job fair, which will depend on their ability to assess candidate quality after only speaking to them briefly.

To increase their odds of learning as much as possible in the short time available at these events, they often inquire, "tell me about yourself" when a candidate approaches their table. The next step for a candidate is contingent upon how well she answers this question. A candidate needs to describe her skills and how she can make an excellent contribution to the company in a very brief time period. If she can present herself effectively, she will be screened in, and scheduled for an interview at a later date.

ADVERTISING

Once upon a time, the most common place to look for a listing of job openings was in the newspaper. For the most part, those days are gone. Print advertising has been declining rapidly in recent years. Although there are still some print ads in local markets, and on a national scale with The Wall Street Journal and The New York Times, most employment advertising has moved to online sources. For those employers who do still utilize print ads, there is a significant cost. These ads can cost thousands of dollars for national publications or hundreds of dollars for local ads.

There are a growing number of online sites where companies can advertise their open jobs by posting them on the site for a fee, based on the number of ads and the length of time the ad(s) run. These ads generally cost in the low hundreds for each advertisement. The sites include monster. com, careerbuilder.com, indeed.org, and others mentioned in Chapter 11. Please review these sites and make sure you have created the appropriate accounts and profiles.

OUTPLACEMENT COMPANY REFERRALS

In this economy, many companies have been forced to cut jobs and lay off employees. In many cases when companies go through this type of downsizing, they refer their laid-off employees to outplacement firms. These firms assist laid-off workers with the job search process and are typically paid 5 percent to 10 percent of payroll to provide a humane approach to assist employees in finding a new job. During this economic period, many excellent employees have been displaced through no fault of their own. Companies can often tap into these very good candidates at no cost.

TEMPORARY HELP AGENCIES

Companies generally use temporary help agencies when they have a short-term need for an employee to complete a specific job. They are often used as a probationary period for a potential new employee, a trial period. In this situation, the company has no obligation to hire if the situation does not work out. In addition, during the temporary employment there are typically no company benefits, which is an added savings for the company. Since the individual is actually employed by the temporary agency, terminating the employee is done by the agency, not the company, which is also a benefit to the company's brand as an employer.

> **Case 4: How Companies Pay Temporary Help Agencies**
>
> *A temporary agency may bill a company $20 per hour for a temporary employee. The temporary employee may receive $15 per hour, and the remaining $5 goes to the temporary agency for payroll tax and other costs, and profit. (This is an over simplification to show in general how these systems work.) Companies are always looking at their temporary employees as potential full-time regular employees. If the temporary employee does a good job in their temporary situation, they can be considered for regular full-time positions.*

EMPLOYMENT AGENCIES

Traditional employment agencies provide a fee-based service to companies. They will recruit and screen candidates for specific open jobs and their average fees to the company will run 20 percent to 25 percent of the employee's starting salary. Employment agencies often run ads in print and online to obtain candidates, and most have extensive files of applicants. Companies will frequently use employment agencies for hard-to-fill openings, or where lower cost recruiting sources haven't worked. Frequently, employment agencies may specialize in key occupational areas and become very good resources for companies and candidates. Sometimes companies can negotiate reduced fees by offering a significant number of open jobs to an agency on an exclusive basis.

EXECUTIVE SEARCH

Executive search firms find senior job candidates for companies. Their targets are generally senior executives who are gainfully employed and not necessarily looking for a job. The search firms will do research on companies and network to find candidates, and most search firms have extensive libraries on corporate information and key candidates. Companies will generally contract with executive search firms for a fee of 30 percent to 35 percent of the first year's compensation plus expenses for screening and interviewing candidates. The company may specify target companies that would provide good candidates. The search firm is obligated to present qualified candidates to earn its fee, regardless of whether or not the company hires one of the candidates. This recruiting resource is a last resort for companies and only used for senior-level jobs, due to the expense.

SCREENING RESUMES

All of the aforementioned sourcing methods result in resumes that must be evaluated and screened. It is imperative that you understand this screening process to best position yourself against competing candidates.

The purpose of this screening process is to review resumes critically to match backgrounds to open job qualifications. The desired outcome of this process is to identify a workable number of candidates who will be evaluated further with the most successful candidates being interviewed in person.

If a small number of resumes are to be screened, a human resources representative will typically go through them and screen in qualified candidates. Some resumes of unqualified candidates, who may be qualified for other positions within the company, are generally held in an electronic hot file. These resumes may be accessed for other open jobs at a later date.

Major companies seeking a large number of candidates to fill open jobs may screen resumes electronically. They use scanning systems that can identify key words or factors in a resume that are qualifications of the job. Such things as technical qualifications, specific experience, education, certifications, supervisory requirements, etc., can be programmed into the scanning system. Resumes that appear to reflect none of the required qualifications are screened out. Depending on other factors on the resume, a few may be placed in a hot file for future openings. The objective in this whole process is to find resumes of individuals who appears to be the most qualified candidates for the open position with the objective of moving forward in the process, most likely to the interview stage.

TELEPHONE OR WEB-BASED VISUAL SCREENS

Typically, candidates who are screened into the process following a resume review will complete a telephone or Skype/FaceTime interview prior to being invited to an on-site interview. These interviews are usually scripted to some extent by the company, to include behavioral questions involving duties and competencies required in the job. There will also be technical questions about the specific job. Often, candidates are asked the same questions as others who are competing for the same position. After all candidates are interviewed in this manner, evaluations are made and the best candidates are invited to a face-to-face interview.

Historically, these screening interviews have been conducted via telephone, but a growing number of companies are using Skype or other web-based visual approaches to screen, so that the candidate can be observed during the process. The candidate is not only being judged on verbal responses but also on appearance and emotional intelligence. A candidate must be prepared for this type of interview by following the steps outlined in Chapter 13.

Nuggets of Wisdom:

- Present the best appearance you can, but remember it is your spirit that counts.

- Learn more than necessary.

- Do not be fooled by your impressions.

- We will eventually lose our good health, but we never have to lose a good attitude.

- The most difficult part of problem solving is identifying the real problem and focusing on what you can change.

- If there is a key to working with others, it is the energy that our behavior carries. Is it fear, threat and attack, or is it caring, acceptance, and support?

Chapter 13

Preparing for a Specific Interview

Outcome:

- I now have a strategy for preparing for a specific interview and I know what will be expected in the interview process.

In Chapter 7 you should have completed a thorough process of interview preparation that focused on your experiences, skills, and talents, in a general sense. This chapter will discuss preparing for a specific interview, which will not be effective if you do not remember the details of your overall interviewing preparation; therefore, if it has been awhile since you read that chapter please spend a few minutes reviewing the information before proceeding.

Now, it is time to discuss the very tactical approach to preparing for a specific interview. In general, assuming that you are completely familiar with your strengths, weaknesses, talents, and gifts, and you have developed a series of "stories" related to your past experience and accomplishments, there are two things you must focus on to prepare for a scheduled interview: 1) the specific job description, and 2) the current condition of the company or organization with which you are interviewing.

ANALYZING THE JOB

Never underestimate the importance of a thorough analysis of a job description or posting. Each one provides clues as to what the recruiter is looking for in a candidate, and what they may ask you. To get a feel for how to conduct this analysis, please read the following Job Posting and then answer the questions asked.

Marketing Coordinator Position
Available in Tampa, Florida

As a Marketing Coordinator you will work closely with our Marketing Directors and Managers to gain valuable experience executing various direct mail and email campaigns. You will be responsible for independently analyzing prospect and customer data; preparing routine reports and correspondence; and administratively aiding in the collection and presentation of data.

- Facilitates marketing campaigns ensuring timely and quality implementation of all related tasks.
- Generates reports with order information and transfers data into marketing analyses.
- Maintains spreadsheets and performs cost analysis of marketing efforts.
- Develops analyses to track the performance of marketing efforts to prospects.
- Manages and maintains product data within company systems.
- Conducts market research to assist in the development and execution of marketing plan objectives.
  Interacts and corresponds with members of the sales, customer service, and editorial teams.

Exercise 1

In Chapter 5, the various Core Competencies sought by most employers were listed, along with questions for you to answer regarding your own skill level. Those competencies are listed below. Circle the five that you believe would be required to do this job effectively and with excellence:

Teamwork	Written Communication
Desire to Learn	Computer Proficiency
Honesty	Flexibility
Work Ethic	Job Desire
Persuasive/Sales Ability	Vision
Rapport Building	Planning/Organization
Creativity/Innovation	Ability to Handle Stress
Problem Solving	Tenacity
Oral Communication	Energy

CUSTOMER ORIENTATION

Now, returning once again to Chapter 5, review your answers to the questions following each of the competencies you circled. Why? Because if these are the competencies the recruiter is looking for, they will certainly want you to discuss your skills in these areas. You must be ready to prove you have what they are looking for if you expect to be hired!

Now, go back to Chapter 7 and review the STAR stories you developed, which focused on the specific accomplishments from your past. Which ones would be most appropriate to prove the competencies you circled above? Are there others you could prepare for this specific interview?

Bottom line? You must determine, by reading the job description and posting, what they are most likely to be looking for and you must be ready to prove you have it! Proving it is essential. You should never just say "yes" to a question about whether or not you have a specific ability. You should ALWAYS give an example – tell your story!

One final point on the job analysis process: In addition to reading the descriptions and postings, if you have access to someone within the organization, try to speak with them about the job and what they believe is the most important trait(s) of the right candidates. This will give you one more layer of information for use in preparing!

UNDERSTANDING THE EMPLOYER/COMPANY/ORGANIZATION

Understanding the current climate in which an employer/company lives is vital. Their current stressors and challenges are likely foremost on their minds, and an appreciation of the impact on both the company and the individual will go a long way in pushing you to the top of the hiring list. You should already be engaging in some "due diligence" ahead of your interview by researching the position and seeking to understand the company, its culture, and employees ahead of your first meeting. You can extend this process by doing your own social listening, or using their digital footprint to get more information and attempt to gauge what they value most, or on how you should position yourself to increase your chances of getting their offer.

By investing some time and effort you can go through a firm's social media presence (LinkedIn, Facebook, Twitter, Instagram, etc.) and take note of their updates, what they choose to share or comment on, and the extent of their activity in general (do they post at all, a little, or a lot). Take note of who they engage with, as well as what they share from other sources. At the very least, this research should give you an idea of how they compete in the marketplace and what sort of value they see themselves as providing to their customers. At this point you should ask yourself how you can contribute to this strategy, and what value you bring to the company – this will be something you'll want to get across during your interview since you are trying to place yourself as the best "product" for them.

With a little more digging you might find other important pieces of information that can be used during the interview. Maybe the company is expanding into a new location, or into a new country. Maybe the president of the company made a recent announcement or statement that impacts the position for which you are interviewing. All of these examples lead to great questions during the interview. For instance, "How will the expansion into XYZ impact my potential duties?" or "With the company moving into XYZ, are there opportunities for me to engage/interact with those managers and learn from their experiences?" or "Considering Mr. CEO's statement last Tuesday, how do you see the growth of the division we're talking about?," etc.

In fact, with enough time and energy, you can employ this approach for the firm's competitors as well to get a more complete understanding of everything the firm is facing.

Whether you choose to engage in social listening or not and how much depends on the type of position you are interviewing for, and who you expect to be interviewing with, since some questions might be appropriate for managers with more intimate knowledge of day-to-day operations. However, the advantage in the approach is clear: demonstrate knowledge about the company, demonstrate interest, and further set yourself apart from other candidates.

Additional social listening can happen in professional social platforms like LinkedIn, where you can turn your focus away from the firm itself and towards its current and former employees. You can use the information contained here to understand the background of their employees or to gauge the common skillsets that lead to, or arise from, employment in the firm. Does it look like a good match from your perspective? Are you bringing something novel or unique to this position? You certainly would want to bring up any of these points in an interview to further highlight the value you potentially bring to the company. Along similar lines, you can attempt to determine an average tenure time for employees in that company. There's a good chance that a company that does not keep employees for more than a few months at a time has some internal/culture problems that are not immediately visible from outside or from asking questions during the interview process. This sort of information could be invaluable to you when choosing the right job offer.

As you do this research and social listening, you will need to track what you learn in some meaningful way so you will be fully prepared as you go into the interview. The planning guides that follow provide basic models for learning about an employer's business and uncovering ways you can best meet their specific needs. Set them up on your laptop computer, in file folders, loose-leaf binders, or in any manner that best suits your working habits. They are meant only to help you get started thinking, learning, and growing with the employer. Please add to the categories and develop your own planning guides.

EMPLOYER GUIDES FOR JOB INTERVIEW PREPARATION

Overall Information

Customer Profile:

Alliances:

Customer's Vision/Overall Goals:

Key Departments/Services:

Key People/Contacts:

Key Competition:

Customer's Major Business Issues/Challenges:

Sales Information

Customer's Target Market/Demographics:

Customer's Competitive Advantages:

Products:

Competitive Products:

Major Supporters for this Customer:

Opportunities and Any Obstacles for Major Product Success:

Factors for Needs of The Customer

Product Benefits of Priority to their Customers:

Needs of their Customer:

Value-Added Services the Company has to Offer:

Business Needs of their Customers that their Value-Added Services can Assist:

Decision-Making Process for Hiring:

How will You Follow Up and Ensure Customer Satisfaction?:

What are You Doing to Build Supportive Relationships with Customer?:

Exercise 2

Using the guide above, research your #1 employer target and fill in the relevant information. Over time, you will need to do this in preparation for every interview, even if you interview with a company that is not on your list.

BACKGROUND CHECKS

Any successful candidate will be required to go through a complete background check. Normally, when you apply to a company or are invited in for an interview, you will be required to fill out a formal application, which is in addition to supplying a resume. The application will require information on your home address; social security number; detailed job experience, including dates, job titles, and salaries; academic record; felony convictions (DWI is a felony in most states); credit information; professional certifications; and any other required information relating to the job.

Included in the application is a legal release form which allows the company to check almost anything related to the qualifications, citizenship, and behavior of the job candidate. This release results in a contract between the candidate and the company, and the candidate certifies that he or she is not lying or misrepresenting anything in his or her background. The release allows for the termination or disqualification of any candidate who lies or misrepresents the information. Many companies will also check social networks, and also do a drug test. It is critical not to lie or misrepresent anything in your background. This will result in termination or disqualification.

Actual Case #1

A graduate school candidate was applying to a major TV company for a business-related position. This candidate had done a great job academically and was one of the leaders of the graduating class. The company was very interested in employing the candidate and indicated that they would do a full background check. The company checked social networks and found postings of the candidate in group activities doing drugs and actively engaging in binge drinking. The company dropped the candidate and moved on to another.

Actual Case #2

A recent college graduate was applying to a company for a professional job. The candidate appeared to have good qualifications and the company made an offer contingent upon passing a background check and a drug test. The background check came out OK, but the drug test showed cannabis. The company terminated the candidate.

Some common reasons for disqualification as an outcome of a background check include:

- Non-US Citizen without proper work permits
- Stolen identity
- Word dates don't check
- Performance feedback from previous employer shows problems
- Academic qualifications don't check
- Poor credit record, particularly for finance or retail jobs
- Felony convictions
- Problematic information on social networking sites
- Failed drug test resulting from using an illegal substance
- Legality in Employment

LEGAL RAMIFICATIONS OF THE INTERVIEW AND THE HIRING PROCESS

Illegal Interview Questions

When a company is making decisions on whether to hire or retain individuals, there are a number of factors that the company must NOT consider. The factors include:

- Race
- Ethnicity
- Sex
- Religion
- Age
- Disability
- National origin
- Marital/family status
- Sexual orientation

Companies should tailor their interview questions to avoid soliciting this information. In addition to raising legal issues, asking such questions could make an interview uncomfortable and create an environment where the candidate performs badly.

Bona Fide Occupational Qualifications

Bona Fide Occupational Qualifications (BFOQ) are qualities or attributes that employers are allowed to consider when making hiring or retention decisions. While these qualities would otherwise amount to discrimination, they are allowable in particular circumstances.

A few examples of BFOQs include:

- Sex-based Hiring: A company that models clothes for a specific gender
- Age-based Hiring/Retention: Mandatory retirement ages for airline pilots

For a qualification to amount to a BFOQ it must be necessary to the normal operation of the company. Mere customer preference for a particular trait does not usually amount to a BFOQ. For instance, customer preference for female flight attendants does not make being a female a BFOQ. Customer preference can only be taken into account when it specifically affects the company's ability to perform its primary function.

Actual Case #1

Hooters is an American restaurant whose wait staff is composed of young females wearing revealing attire. Hooters has faced multiple challenges that it engages in sex discrimination in its hiring process. As a defense, Hooters argued that femininity is a BFOQ. Is hiring young females reasonably necessary to the operation of Hooters? May Hooters consider customer preference for attractive young female waitresses? What is the primary essence of Hooters' business?

According to the two rulings following two separate lawsuits brought by men claiming discrimination, one in 1997 and another in 2009, Hooters can use femininity as a BFOQ because it is considered to be the essence of their business.

Lying on a Resume

Some states have enacted statutes that deem resume fraud a criminal offense; however, these statutes are narrowly applied. In these states it is illegal to utilize a false degree issued by a "diploma mill' to procure employment. "Diploma mills" refer to unaccredited institutions that often hand diplomas to any paying customer. Aside from this narrow prohibition, no US laws criminalize lying on an employment resume. That said, lying or misrepresenting employment or educational history, licensure or expertise, may amount to just-cause for termination.

Actual Case #2

An individual applying to become president of a software company made multiple misrepresentations on his resume. In addition to lying about his educational credential, he also falsified information regarding his military background and his expertise in Tae Kwon Do. Could an employer consider any of these misrepresentations in terminating an individual?

Yes, all of these could be grounds for termination, depending upon the hiring laws of the state and on whether or not the falsification is considered "material." Materiality depends on the satisfaction of two conditions.

1. The falsification must be firstly related to a requirement for employment.

2. The employer must rely on the falsified information when making the hiring decision.

When such conditions are satisfied, the falsification is deemed material and an employer has just-cause to terminate the employee.

DISCRIMINATION IN THE WORKPLACE

Federal and state laws, particularly in the last few decades, have attempted to curb discrimination in the workplace. Such laws have addressed the following types of discrimination.

- **Sex discrimination.** Sexual discrimination statutes aim to prevent a hostile work environment for all genders and gender identification. Additionally, the Pregnancy Discrimination Act mandated that pregnancy and related conditions be treated like other temporary conditions or illnesses.

- **Religious discrimination.** An employer must make reasonable accommodations for an employee's religious beliefs, unless doing so would pose an undue hardship.

- **Disability discrimination.** Under the Americans with Disabilities Act (ADA), an individual with a disability is someone with: 1) a physical or mental impairment that substantially limits a major life activity, 2) someone with a record of such impairment, or 3) someone who is regarded as having a disability. An individual with a disability is qualified for a job if they possess the skill, experience, education, and other job-related requirements for the position. Such an individual must be able to perform the key functions of that position, with or without reasonable accommodation. An employer is required to make reasonable accommodations for a qualified individual with a disability unless doing so would pose undue hardship. Undue hardship amounts to a significant difficulty or expense for an employer, with consideration of the business' resources and size.

- **Age discrimination.** An employer is prevented from imposing age specifications, preferences, or limits for employment unless age amounts to a BFOQ. Additionally, statues protect older employees from being denied benefits.

- **Equal wages.** The law seeks to ensure that men and women are paid equally when performing work of similar effort, skill, and responsibility under similar work conditions.

Nuggets of Wisdom

- Be sure to thank the administrative assistant and/or receptionist when you leave following an on-site interview.

- Celebrate progress and achievement. Of the two, progress is more important.

- Judge your performance by results, quality, and enjoyment.

- Find out when and where you are when you feel the most creative.

- Get a haircut or shave if you feel you probably should.

- If you wonder if a certain outfit is appropriate for an interview, change into something that you know, for certain, is.

- Read a book on how to dress successfully.

- Provide the little touches, like a hand written thank-you note.

- Learn something about the area or town before you interview in a new place.

Chapter 14

Assessing the Offers and Negotiating the Deal

Outcomes:

- I now have an understanding of how to assess all job offers I have received and negotiate the best deal possible for me and for my future.

JOB OFFERS

Once all interview are complete, and background checks have been finalized, a successful candidate will receive a job offer, which is, of course, the objective and goal from the onset. Typically, the initial offer will be verbal, generally followed by a letter or email that outlines the specifics of the offer. The initial offer may include:

- Starting salary
- Bonus or incentive eligibility, if applicable
- Job title
- Starting date of employment
- Probationary periods of job
- Location of work assignment and where and who to report to
- Outline of any relocation assistance
- Start date of benefit coverage
- Any special issues concerning the job

The verbal offer is usually followed by a written offer that outlines all of the provisions of the job situation in more detail.

This will/should include:

- Copy of the job description

- Copies of benefit plans

- Rules and regulations that apply to the job

- Company business and policy information

- Other material related to the company and the job

The written offer may also include a request for additional information from the candidate such as a birth certificate, driver's license, social security card, proof of military service, and/or any other information used in the company's verification process. Some companies will collect pieces of this information during the final interview phase, but be prepared to provide additional documentation as requested, either at the time of acceptance or when you begin work. Also, please note the offer letter will require that you return a copy of the letter to the company with your signature of acceptance. This results in your first contractual agreement with the company.

Negotiating the Job Offer

The opportunity to negotiate the job offer happens after the verbal offer, and this is the only chance you'll get so you need to be prepared. Of course, if the offer and all provisions of the offer are satisfactory, you should immediately accept the position and thank the company verbally and with a written reply to the individual who extended the offer. However, if for some reason the offer doesn't meet your expectations, you have an opportunity to engage in "respectful negotiations."

Setting the stage for respectful negotiations begins with a heartfelt thank you when you receive the verbal offer, along with a request for time to review the verbal and written offers. Most companies will give you a week or two of extension to finalize your acceptance or rejection of the job offer. After that they will press you for an answer. Employers recognize that if a candidate does not accept immediately there may be some issues or problems with the offer. They may also suspect that the candidate has other offer(s) to consider.

Various issues can trigger a candidate's desire to negotiate. These include, but are not limited to, the following:

- Offer salary is too low. Usually the college office of career management will have a good picture of the market and the average salaries for different types of graduates.

- The candidate needs time to consider other offers, some of which may be coming later.

- The candidate has a lot of related job experience that isn't being recognized in the offer.

- The job involves relocation, and there is no relocation assistance.

- The job involves relocation to a major market that has significantly higher living costs.

- Geographical limitations of the job present problems.

- Requirements of a probationary period had not been previously discussed.

- Job requirements include unanticipated travel.

- Candidate has a valid conflict with the start date (wedding planned, summer military duty, or something else very important).

- There may be other important issues in the offer that were not previously discussed.

Please take note of the following unacceptable reasons to negotiate:

- Need the summer off to go on vacation after graduating

- Not enough vacation time from the company

- Work hours appear to be too long

- Job duties are too difficult

The most common reason for negotiating an offer centers on the salary and/or the need for time to consider another offer(s). Keep in mind that the employer has made an offer to you, has probably completed a full background check, and has already determined that they want you to work in their company. At this point, you have the leverage and, if you need to, this is the time for you to have a respectful negotiation.

To be fully prepared for this, you should do your homework. If the issue is salary, gather the resources that will support your request for a higher salary. Talk to your office of career management and/or use appropriate internet resources to determine appropriate salary ranges for the position and the area. Look online at the rates for college graduates in markets similar to where you will be working. (Keep in mind that if you have more experience than the average graduate, you have a basis to ask for higher salary consideration). The rates are higher in the major cities, perhaps by as much as 10% to 30%. Regardless of the issue, you must do your homework and get the facts before you negotiate.

Generally, when you are ready to negotiate, you contact the individual who made the offer to you in the first place. Have a fact-based conversation that will politely demonstrate you have done your homework. The specifics should indicate that the reasons you are asking for additional consideration are valid. You really have nothing to lose, and the worst thing that could happen is the company will not make a change in your terms and conditions of employment.

Thinking Like the Employer

In conclusion, let's take a minute to "think like the employer" which will provide you with a framework as you head into the negotiations. Remember that employers have a lot to consider when a candidate asks for more money. Organizations that hire college graduates are generally very aware of the salaries being offered to graduates because they share the information with each other and talk to the various career offices. They have an excellent understanding of the market and make their offers based on that knowledge.

One key issue has to do with the college graduates they hired last year. Usually larger employers will hire numerous college graduates each year and they typically bring them in at a similar salary level. For example, imagine that a major company brought in several accounting graduates last year at $48,000. Each of them received a cost of living increase, so the average salary of the group is $51,000. To maintain a level of fairness, the employer will not bring in new hires at salaries that get too close to $51,000. The maximum they are likely to offer is $49,000 to $50,000, unless a candidate has exceptional experience or is in the top 5% of the class. You must know this information, and consider all of the potential ramifications as you begin the negotiating process.

With this in mind, knowing some of the top candidates are going to require additional monetary incentives, employers will sometimes have flexibility with up-front bonuses or one-time payments for something specific. It is much easier for a company to make an up-front one-time payment that increases a base salary offer.

Case: A Typical Salary Negotiation

A graduating business student in Tennessee had a verbal offer of $42,000 from a company in Chicago that appeared to be a little low. The offer did not include any relocation assistance. The human resources representative extended the offer via telephone. The job candidate thanked the HR officer and told him that she loved the company and all the people she met there, but asked for a week to review the offer. The candidate was concerned that the dollar offer might not be enough to rent an apartment and help her move to Chicago. She did her homework and found that Chicago had a higher cost of living and apartments were 20% higher than Knoxville, Tennessee. She also estimated her moving costs, and felt that she needed at least $3,000 a year more in salary. At the end of the week, she called the human resources representative for the company and told him she was very interested in the company, but needed some consideration for the financial issues that she researched. She had a respectful conversation by outlining the facts. The company told her that they could not be flexible on base salary because it would impact other recent graduates they were hiring as well as the graduates they hired last year. They said they could offer her an up-front bonus of $8,000 in recognition of the fact she was moving from Knoxville to Chicago. The candidate accepted the bonus and moved to Chicago.

One last reminder, if you want to negotiate with an employer, it must be done respectfully. You must do your homework and present a polite case, with a factual backup. You can't negotiate for more just because you want more. Also, remember that the company has offered you a job. They want you! Consequently, the only downside is that they say no to your request. There is no harm in trying if you have a legitimate case.

Nuggets of Wisdom

- Be open and candid about the compensation system.

- Look at any problem and make a decision to embrace it.

- Nothing is as easy as it looks.

- Everything takes longer than it ought to.

- Ask for what you want.

- Take risks.

Chapter 15

Transitioning to the Job

Outcome:

- I now know the main things I need to consider as a transition into a new job.

If you are reading this, and are truly transitioning into a job, congratulations! If you are still waiting to secure a position, please take to heart the guidance that is provided.

EXERCISE 1

In the movie *Love Affair*, Kathryn Hepburn stated, "A happy life is not having everything you want – it is wanting everything you have."

What is your gut reaction to this quote?

Give a real example of how it applies to you in your job.

How does it apply in your non-work related life?

What other questions, thoughts, or feelings do you have about this quote?

Understanding what true contentment is, and learning how to reach certain milestones in your life leading to contentment, is crucial to job satisfaction and success. Even as you transition now into a new role, approaching it with this mindset will have a huge impact. To that end, you must aggressively learn more about the company that has hired you, focusing on their vision, mission statement, goals, values, customers, challenges, problems, and opportunities. In light of these, you must quickly begin to understand your specific responsibilities, the outcomes expected from you, and how you will be evaluated.

As you begin this new journey, it is important to keep in mind that the "interview" continues, at least for a while. As you are adjusting to the new job, and trying to find a work/life balance that truly leads to contentment, remember that you ended up at this place because someone or a group of individuals gave you an opportunity and took a risk on you. Their examination of you and your abilities will continue for quite some time.

As you start your new job, you are most likely on a spoken or an unspoken probation or trial period for three to six months. You now have the opportunity to prove you have what it takes to do the job you have been hired to do, and that you have all the skills and competencies you told them about in the interview process.

To fully maximize this probationary period, please remember that you will be watched very closely so that the following can be fully assessed:

- Your work ethic
- Your eagerness and curiosity to learn
- Your meeting or exceeding expectations (standards)
- Your ability to work with others

Simultaneously, it will be crucial that you begin to understand your direct supervisor or manager. This is important, obviously, because you need to know what this individual expects and learn about his or her management style. Equally important, however, is an understanding of how well this individual is likely to meet your needs, and how they may cause you stress. Remember that rare is the manager who will meet all of your needs or, in some cases, even care that you have them. You must understand these needs, ask for what you need, or recognize that, at times, they won't be met, depending upon the situation and the manager. Obviously, for all of us, there are situations that are simply intolerable. Hopefully, through the guidance laid out in this book, you have vetted all of your opportunities and are in a job that closely aligns with your overall needs and strengths.

Let's revisit your Birkman results in light of what you need from others, including whoever is your boss. We will look at two different reports here to gain a fuller understanding of what you need individually from your manager, specifically in communication, and what you need in general terms to stay appropriately motivated.

Please locate and read Topic 2, "How to Talk to Him/Her" and Topic 16, the report titled "Motivating for Best Performance."

While we won't do a formal exercise here, please read these carefully and refer back to them as needed throughout the first few months of your new job. It is inevitable that some of these needs will not be met on a consistent basis, but knowing what they are can help you avoid derailing reactions.

Remember, now that you are employed your primary customer is your new boss, as well as your co-workers. Your immediate supervisor deserves your loyalty, commitment, and desire to learn and move the entire organization forward. In this context, your most valuable asset is your credibility or integrity. Don't do anything that would jeopardize or lessen either. Make and keep promises!

- Be on time. (10 minutes before the appointed time.)

- Perform your responsibilities, duties, and administrative requirements.

- Work hard and be ready to spend time on what is necessary. (Be engaged in your job.)

- Learn.

- Do what you said you would do when you were interviewed.

Finally, it will be your responsibility, and yours alone, to determine what aspects of your Birkman results you share with your new manager. The results of your answers to The Birkman Method® have pointed out many of your strengths and weaknesses that you and your manager can build upon, but you will need to be savvy in determining what to share and when to share it.

That said, even if you choose to share none of your results directly with your supervisor, you need to spend some time reviewing your results in light of your performance at work, and in light of your potential reaction to the stress that will inevitably come with a new position. The following section will guide you through specific reports and topics that deal with some of these areas, and we encourage you to spend some introspective time considering these reports.

Managing What's Next

1. **Leveraging Strengths and Interests.** Ideally, your new position is leveraging both your strengths and interests, but in many entry level jobs, things may be asked of you that leverage neither. Some call this "paying your dues." In reality, it is usually an organization's design and will require patience and diligence on your part. None of us want to do things we don't enjoy, or don't feel play to our strengths, but for most of us, it is necessary at times. What we are asking here is that you simply review what your strengths and interests are so you will be ready to talk about them and utilize them, even if you are not asked to do so. Doing more than you are asked to do is the key to moving into a role down the line that will leverage these areas more effectively. With that in mind, locate and read the following reports. Familiarize

yourself with these again, and think about how they can now play into success in your new role.

Please locate and read Topics 11-14, "The Effects of Interests on Work," "Your Strengths," "His/Her Management Style," and "His/Her Leadership Style."

2. **Trust and Influence.** In order for this new position to lead to success for you, and your employer, you must build and maintain trust with you new boss and co-workers. People approach this trust-building process in all sorts of ways, but in the end, the way you communicate and choose to influence others will have a huge impact on how you establish trust. The Birkman Method® provides a nice roadmap for this by highlighting your effective ways of communicating and influencing. Familiarize yourself with this information and then use it to build the bridges and relationships you will need to be highly effective and successful.

Please locate and read Topic 3, "How He/She Handles People," Section 1, When He/She is at His/Her Best."

Also locate and read Topic 8, "How He/She Seeks to Influence Others, Section 1: His/Her Effective Approach."

3. **Motivating for best performance.** As we have discussed throughout this book, each of us is motivated in very unique and personal ways. Many of us wallow in job dissatisfaction when we are not feeling motivated, and for the most part, can't put our finger on what the specific de-motivators are, which leaves us feeling helpless. If you truly understand what does motivate you, it will be much easier to recognize what is missing and avoid that feeling of helplessness. Arm yourself with this information!

Please locate and read Topic 16, "Motivating for Best Performance."

4. **Handling Conflict.** Conflict in any organization is inevitable, and the way you handle it begins to define you as a professional. Some of us wear our feelings on our sleeves, and doing so can be viewed as unprofessional. Others tend to disregard the feelings or opinions of others during confrontational moments, which can also be viewed as unprofessional. Please keep your tendencies in mind as you move into this new phase of your life, clearly understanding that moving "up" in an organization often depends on how you manage these types of situations.

Please locate and read Topic 19, "Conflict." Please read Sections A, B, and C.